REFLECTIONS OF A PUBLIC SERVANT

REFLECTIONS
OF A PUBLIC SERVANT

End of a Journey

by

Charles P. Messick

Foreword by William W. Boyer

Charles P. Messick Professor
of Public Administration
University of Delaware

UNIVERSITY OF DELAWARE

Newark, Delaware

PREVIOUS BOOKS BY THE AUTHOR:

An Adventure in Public Personnel Administration (1973)

The Principles of Public Personnel Administration (1976)

The Passing Scene: A Commentary on Public Affairs (1976)

Contents

Foreword

This is the fourth book produced by Dr. Charles Polk Messick within the span of five years, no mean feat for a man of 95 years of age. Dr. Messick died March 22, 1978, as this book was in press. Thinking of this book as his last, he considered entitling it "End of a Journey." I prevailed on him, however, to entitle it otherwise, because I knew him as one who would doubtlessly continue to devote himself selflessly to the improvement of the quality of life of his nation and people until his last breath. He was that kind of man; such was his energy and creativity. After his death, I took the liberty of acceding to his wish, as this last effort truly represents the end of a remarkable journey.

The following are excerpts from my introduction to his first book, published in 1973, which now appear as sort of an epitaph. At that time, I wrote:

"Few of his contemporaries can combine so many enriching roles of public service as, for example, those of teacher, educator, lecturer, public administrator, author, businessman and banker — any one of which would be satisfying and challenging enough for ordinary mortals. But Dr. Messick is no ordinary mortal.

"He was born in Sussex County, Delaware, on June 1, 1882. After earning his bachelor's degree in 1907 and a master's degree in 1909 at Delaware College — now the University of Delaware — and another master's degree in 1910 at the University of Pennsylvania, young Charles Messick moved to New Jersey, first to teach at Wenonah Military Academy and then to head the history department at Trenton High School. It was in New Jersey that he was destined to become not only one of that state's most distinguished citizens but, indeed, the very embodiment of a state institution.

"He joined the New Jersey State Civil Service Commission as a special examiner in 1910 and served as assistant chief examiner of the Commission from 1912-1917. In the latter capacity, he developed the work of the examining department to a high level, attracting the attention of public personnel leaders in all parts of the United States and beyond. But it was during his long tenure of 32 years as the Commission's chief examiner and secretary, from 1917 to 1949, that Dr. Messick received unique state and national recognition and honors for his exemplary public service in New Jersey.

"When Dr. Messick first entered public personnel administration, only a few states and large cities were struggling to establish civil service systems predicated on a negative 'keep-the-rascals (i.e. politicians) out' philosophy. Dr. Messick never accepted such negative arguments in support of civil service. Instead he advocated civil service for better government — as a positive contribution toward professionalization of the public service. It is this positive philosophy that has become widely accepted by public officials, personnel administrators, and citizens alike throughout the United States.

"Today, all of our 50 states operate under some form of a state-wide merit system. Moreover, many of our 185,000 local governments scattered throughout the United States, and especially those with populations of 50,000 or more, operate under merit systems.

"Much of this achievement can be attributed to the seminal leadership of Dr. Charles Messick. Not only did he devote his constant attention to improvement of public personnel administration in New Jersey, but his leadership was decisive in public personnel organizations throughout the United States. He was organizer and chairman of the Board of Trustees of the Bureau of Public Personnel Administration that served as the headquarters staff of the Civil Service Assembly of the United States and Canada, later the large and powerful Public Personnel Association.* He served the Civil Service Assembly re-

---

* The Public Personnel Association became the International Personnel Management Association in 1973.

peatedly in every office and on every important committee, including the offices of vice president, president, and member and chairman of the executive council for many years.

"A faithful public servant and a prolific author, lecturer and consultant on public personnel administration, Charles Messick was awarded honorary doctorates by the University of Delaware, Rutgers University and Rider College. His influence and counsel were not confined to public personnel administration, however, but reached nearly every important public activity in New Jersey. A modern Benjamin Franklin, he was renowned as a sort of combined father confessor, counsellor, and consultant for everybody — including governors and legislators — in official or semiofficial public positions in New Jersey. He is reputed to have written more state papers in New Jersey than any other living person."

This present volume opens with some of Dr. Messick's retrospective remarks, which are followed by his 1938 address before the Civil Service Assembly, a chapter from a 1940 book on public management (both of which are still as pertinent today), his contemporary narrative about the ground-breaking merit system in New Jersey, his 1966 address before the Public Personnel Association's 60th anniversary meeting, his 1976 address before the 70th anniversary meeting of its successor International Personnel Management Association, and ends with an epilogue with verse.

This book is a further testament to the veracity of my concluding observations in the introduction to his 1973 book, namely: "Few Americans since the beginning of our Republic can match the record of high citizenship and distinguished public service established by Dr. Charles P. Messick."

> William W. Boyer
> *Charles P. Messick Professor*
> *of Public Administration*
> *University of Delaware*

Newark, Delaware
March 1978

Preface

In my third book, *The Passing Scene: A Commentary on Public Affairs*, I wrote that as a young teacher, with little knowledge of the techniques and methods of teaching, I soon discovered that those who attempt to teach others must be masters of the subject in the grade in which they are teaching, and that as I advanced in the profession, I found that the same principle prevailed in writing and in every activity relating to both teaching and learning. I looked forward to the time when I would be able to speak convincingly and write sufficiently well to have those writings accepted and the proposals therein be of some value to beginners in the field and possibly to some who had some experience in the art themselves.

The principle involved here is no new thing or proposal. I neither claim its discovery nor even claim emphasizing it. It is to my mind merely a simple truth. I gave a copy of the book in which I had stated the above fact, as I saw and had experienced it, to some of my friends for their inspection and criticism.

The relevant statement as it appeared in the introduction of the book is: "I have talked to all kinds of audiences on many kinds of subjects, large and small, including audiences in ten or more of our great colleges and universities. I claim no success, but one thing I know that the speaker must possess. He must know what he is talking about. The same principle applies with equal force in writing. I say from my own experience that hard work is more dependable than inspiration, valuable as that may be, and knowledge is more dependable than hope, as essential as that may be." I need to add nothing more to this statement, but I can say that I know what hard work is. It has been of my long experience.

A number of those who read the book had comments to share. Doctor Fred P. Carson, formerly President of Dickinson College in Carlisle, Pennsylvania, and later Bishop of the Methodist Episcopal Church in the Philadelphia District, found something in this statement that attracted his attention. He wrote me and we later talked about it several times, and he insisted that my frank statement should be extended into a new book since few if any speakers and writers have been brave enough to make a statement like this, that it marks a new issue and must be exploited. He called it a new law, a Messick Law.

I have throughout my long career been careful in what I say to others, and in dealing with public officials from constables to presidents one must know what he is talking about and when and how to present it. The Bishop has been through all of these things much more than I. He had both executive and scholarly ability to contend with, and much the same in his Bishopric. Even in his retirement he served his church by travelling up and down America visiting his peers, helping here, encouraging there, challenging elsewhere as the situation demanded. I could not resist his continuous insistence. Hence this fourth book.

I question the wisdom of my actions in this effort but there is some chance in the matter and as I begin I think of some verse. Who may have authored it is unknown. He left without leaving his mark.

Isn't it strange that captains and kings
And clowns who caper in sawdust rings
And common folk like you and me
Are builders for eternity.
To each is given a kit of tools
A shapeless mass and a book of rules
And each must build ere life is done
A stumbling block or a stepping stone.

As I look around, backward, forward, even over some of the wrongs and errors we, the people, as individuals and as a body, make every day, it does give me pause. Some wonder if we can survive as a society and a nation. But then I remember that crises are daily occurrences and after all we make progress by and through them. Changes come by way of crises. People who are standing by and waiting do little. We move ahead as we organize, as we follow a leader. In that way we get a new, or at least another, deal and finally the warring ceases. The waters of hate and fear subside. We have made some progress, and so the story goes.

The Bishop's statement is pertinent and convincing. I am not so sure that I can call the statement I spoke and wrote a New Law. Modernists would likely call it a syndrome. Changes are needed and we of today must make them. We can do so if we mix our plans and efforts with some patience and understanding and will advance step by step toward the goals we seek at the end of the journey.

I am grateful to Dr. William W. Boyer, Messick Professor of Public Administration at the University of Delaware, for helping me put this book together. I also wish to acknowledge the able editorial assistance of Elise Harvey.

Rehoboth, Delaware
December 1977

CHAPTER 1

In Retrospect

To explain our present to ourselves and to others, we look
back. We know what has gone before in our memories. If we
wish or need to go beyond that, we read history. Ten years ago
I was invited to return to my adopted state of New Jersey where
I lived for sixty years of my working life to talk about the begin-
nings and the development of what was then a new conception
of personnel management in which I was fortunate enough to
discuss and test my methods in reaching that conception and to
apply to and in the public service of the state and its subordinate
jurisdictions. It is only fair and factual to record that the experi-
mental work I did there became and yet remains the pattern for
all America. I became the leader of the profession in the field and
I had the satisfaction of serving my state and the nation in this
function of the difficult and understanding problems of administrative management.

This statement is not to be interpreted as a claim to superior or unusual knowledge or vainglory. I was not alone in devising the procedures. There were others in the field who had done
well in meeting the same difficulties and procedures that I faced
and had done well in their efforts. I picked out the situations that

1

they were able to meet, studied the methods that they had used and wove them into my own procedures, and in this way I found the way to success.

I have spent the most of my working life in the study, the place and the part of the personnel who do the work of government, and no small part of that time has been spent in studying the quality of those who direct that personnel and the affairs of the government itself. In New Jersey I spent more of my time with and in the executive and the legislative branches than in the personnel management part itself. I succeeded in gaining the confidence of governors regardless of their politics or the political situations. I did the same thing for the legislature, their committees, and special commissions of all kinds; planned their investigations; wrote their reports; and explained and defended their findings and their proposals. Politics was not adjourned but there was an era of good feeling. There are none left who were active in the inner circle who can agree or dispute what I have written here. It is, however, a simple fact. I do not expect to see it again.

As I write, there is bitterness, suspicion, revolt and war throughout the world. Life and property are not safe and crime drives our highways and walks our streets unafraid. Nevertheless, people are again awake and they are moving back toward better days. Progress and unity, peace and prosperity are moving back to their places here at home and slowly but steadily in many areas of the world.

In retrospect, as it is always difficult to instigate new and different administrative policies whether they are good or bad, change always brings differences. We were trying to install merit for indifference, and ability for inability. It has been done but public opinion and power is not easily overcome. There is no need for proof. As a nation we have lived over two hundred years. We are far from our ideals. We are not good enough to feel comfortable in going on as we are and not bad enough to give up trying in our public affairs.

For many years, I have been emphasizing the fact that government, good or bad, can be no better and no worse than those who direct its affairs and do its work. And therein lie all the facts of the operators and the prophets. The way to reach that goal is to take the steps that must be taken to achieve that goal. We know the road; we know the way to go; what we lack is the impetus, the spirit, to take the steps to travel the highway and to go on to reach the goals. All these require no new discoveries, no new testing, no new proofs. It is we the people who fail, not the knowledge nor the theory. Will it come about by calm effort, the putting into effect by our calm judgment and common sense, or by disorder and revolution? I have been studying this problem for over seventy years.

Beginning a section of a book and ending it with the same subject is not merely a practice, it is a necessity. Everything that is spoken or written is, in substance, education in respect to some additional knowledge about, or for or against something. However much we may have read and thought about things, problems or situations, we have not completed our knowledge. When we no longer read or think, we live in a vacuum. We exist only.

In spite of our concern, we are constantly questioning what education is and how to attain it for ourselves or for others — all of us. The dictionary does not help us very much. It tells us how to get it but not exactly what it is, that is to say, when a person is educated. We find that education, according to the dictionary is: the process of training and developing the knowledge, skill, of mind or character by formal schooling or study; to teach, instruct. An educator is one who instructs others in some of these skills. If we insist on the answer to the question of who may be called an educated person and when, we have no answer. We might add that one is educated when he is aware of the world about us and the people around us. After all, it does not matter too much whether we base our training of children on showing them things and explaining their use as the child grows, and teaching them words and their meaning, their application and use in life or whether we go back to the scholars and philosophers of the ages and build our education on that foundation.

Education is the greatest concern of our lives. It begins at birth and ends the last day of life. We try to define it. We talk about it continually. We spend time and money on it, and we have not yet found the way to educate our people that is satisfactory to all of us. We cannot agree; as a matter of fact we do not know when and at what stage in his life one can be said to have or possess an education.

In our search for correct answers to these questions we have found some landmarks and guidelines to our educational system of today, as we move along toward our ideals. To realize the complete answer we cannot and should not rely on the educators alone. They must carry the greater part of the load, but they have as partners, in the effort, the parents, the several professional groups, the government at its several levels and the people as a whole.

The teachers as a matter of fact know more about the business of teaching and educational procedures than anyone else. They ask that they be left to themselves to plan and apply these procedures leading, in their judgment, to the desired end. In my early years as a teacher I stood with them, but even then, as my experience increased, I had an uneasy feeling that some parts of their developing plans and conclusions were open to question. As time passed, that suspicion hardened into conviction.

In my later years as a member and sometimes president of the Board of Education of Trenton, New Jersey, and active in the public affairs of the city and state, I saw what seemed to me a number of weak spots and actions that were wrong in themselves and contrary to the tested and better ways of dealing with the problems of the people, including our public education.

I yet stood with the teachers. I remember their problems with some of our board members whom I had taught in high school. We yet placed teachers and education high on our list. We asked for and got, both local and statewide, respect and consideration for our teachers, adequate pay, promotion as warranted, a career service, and retirement pay sufficient to permit them to live in comfort and quiet dignity when their work was done.

It is not an easy thing for me to say, but I would be less than truthful if I did not say that the teachers have failed us in no small measure. They have joined the working forces of our whole economy by demanding the right to write the terms and conditions upon which they will continue to perform their duties, and have joined the organized workers throughout the world in the use of the raw force of the strike unless their demands are met.

The strike, however much or extensive and effective it is, is not the final answer to our human problems. No one is wise enough to forecast its end. Teachers have accepted it but in so doing have destroyed themselves as teachers. They teach the history of this nation and the countries of the world, the story of the founding fathers who pledged their lives, their fortune, and their honor for the creation and acceptance of our charter of liberty and freedom and individual opportunity. The strike is an instrument of force. The country has managed to live with it thus far, but that is no assurance that it will continue on indefinitely.

There are, however, two parts of our whole political economy that cannot go farther, and these are our civil servants and our teachers. These must continue in their functions every day; the teachers, for our youth, the civil servants, because government must go on every day and every hour; its stoppage at any time spells disaster. The news media has recently announced that the leader of one of the large union organizations has proposed that the rank and file of the armed forces be unionized.

I recognize that the foregoing observation is a depressing picture, but there is a brighter side in the offing that gives us some relief. The sun is breaking through the clouds. There are some great teachers yet at their daily work and others are following. One of the greatest of these was William Lyon Phelps, who wrote:

> I had rather earn my living by teaching than in any other way. To my mind teaching is not merely a life work, a profession, an occupation, a struggle; it is a passion. I love to teach as a painter loves to paint, as a musician loves to play, as a singer loves to sing, as a strong man rejoices to run a race. Teaching is an Art so great and so difficult to master that a man or a woman can spend a long life at it without realizing much more than his limitations and his mistakes; and his distance from the ideal. But the main aim of my happy days has been to become a good teacher just as every good architect wishes to be a good architect and every professional poet strives toward perfection.

Of all the statements I have heard or read, this to my mind is the best. It is perfection personified, a level that can

5

hardly be reached and never excelled, by us, or so far as I can see in the prospects ahead.

As citizens, we have made progress; as parents, we have contributed our part; as teachers, we have failed to demonstrate and maintain the high standards that are possible and within our grasp. Yet it must be that we will awake again to our old selves as dedicated and devoted teachers to our work and our responsibilities.

Men and women will again become active in service and loyalty, and the old America will live again, when all shall work not for themselves alone but for the people and the state. But with this hopeful forecast we must not forget the dangers that lurk in the background. We are reckless spenders; we buy whatever strikes our fancy, pay whatever may be the price and charge it to our grandchildren. We have wasted a great proportion of our national resources; many of them will take generations to replace and others are irreplacable. We who have run the race can raise the flag of trouble and danger as we take our seat by the side of the road and warn those who are on the march, but that does not relieve us of the damages that have been done. We can only warn our successors, with the hope that they will listen.

CHAPTER 2

Consolidating the Gains*

Back in the days of our simplicity, before we learned that work is waste and New England thrift foolish extravagance, those of us who gathered in groups like this indulged in some anxiety about the burden of government and speculated upon our capacity as a people to maintain a satisfactory level of good administration. We offered, as our contribution, the acceptance of the theory, and the application of the practice, of better man management in public affairs. The storms came. And there is a new dispensation in our whole public economy. But our thesis stands. Indeed it has grown and flourished like the "Green Bay Tree" (that was the tree that flourished, was it not?). Better public personnel and better management of that personnel are now acknowledged to be fundamental essentials of good administration. We are short on acceptance of these essentials, to be sure, but we loyally proclaim them.

It has become the fashion not only for reformers, high-minded citizens and business leaders to endorse merit and career systems in government, but governors, legislators, politicians and statesmen now declare in their favor and give them intermittent

---

* Address at a meeting of the Eastern Regional Conference Area of the Civil Service Assembly of the United States and Canada, in Massachusetts, in May 1938.

7

comfort and support. The brave dream of that little group of devoted men who first gathered here in New England fifty-seven years ago seems about to come true. This must be especially pleasing to the people of Massachusetts because some of the citizens of this commonwealth took, at the beginning and have continued to take, an important part in the whole civil service reform movement. It is not politic, of course, to say harsh things even though they be true. It is to be regretted, however, and New Englanders must share also in this sentiment, that all of the states and cities in New England did not translate that early enthusiasm into practical and effective administrative action and take the lead in demonstrating to all the country that good public personnel administration must be the constant companion and co-partner of good government.

I would not undertake to say that those who are represented in this group and in our National Assembly are responsible for the changes that have taken place in public thinking in recent years, but I like to think that those of us who have worked together during the last quarter of a century have given power and direction and practical application to this popular movement toward a better public personnel.

Surprised as many people have been at the recent far-reaching changes that have taken place in public thinking and in citizen attitude toward public personnel management, it seems to me that these changes are almost obvious. Certainly this is so if we examine the situation a little. Government, or that system of restraints and regulations that men acting together have placed upon themselves in denial or in support of what is conceived to be for the welfare of the group, has been the greatest factor in the development of the arts of civilization.

It is the joint heritages, not individual accomplishment, that are preserved and woven into the customs and thinking of the people. They are fostered and maintained by the presence of government, and they are most valuable and significant in the progress of the nations. If this has not seemed to be true in America heretofore, it is obviously so today. Certainly government has now reached, in America, new and heretofore untried levels in its concern for the welfare of all of the people. We are under no compulsion to like, or to believe in, the things that our government is now undertaking to make this acknowledgement. We need only to recognize the things that are before our eyes — the manifestations of these undertakings of government we see day after day in all their ramifications and implications.

Government has assumed the role of trying to do more generally for the people, all of them, than the family, the community, the group or any sector or part of the people are undertaking to do on their own account. This philosophy of the role of government is not new doctrine, but it is new to the American people in the regulation of their own affairs. It may be the correct and the logical course for us to take. Under it government may be able to accomplish the broad objectives sought and to maintain its character of beneficience, but it is paternalistic government and new to our American ways and our old habits of thought. Without much understanding of the basic changes that are here involved or the possible end results, it seems to me the American people seek for the moment what seems to them to be security rather than to assume the old risks of individual resourcefulness and individual enterprise. For the first time in our whole history, perhaps, the desire for security is stronger than the desire for free choice or for equality.

I am not going to try to tell you whether these new theories and practices, new to us at least, are wise or unwise, whether they will work or fail. First, because I do not know; second, because I am not supposed to be talking about this subject anyway; and third, because all of you know the answers already and probably none of you agree in your conclusions. This we do know, however. Regardless of our individual notions and convictions, and regardless of the failure or partial failure of some or many of these new public commitments, many of these expanded functions of government and new governmental undertakings, either in their present or in some other form, are bound to be continued. The best government from now on will not be considered as that which does the least but that which does a great many things for the people and does them with reasonable effectiveness.

Our old political economy (now adjourned) taught us

that government moved in cycles, from absolutism to limited monarchy to democracy and so on. And this is only another way of saying that the habits and thoughts and actions of men move along the same pattern. If we accept history, changes will take place much in the same way now and for the future as heretofore. This phenomenon is not peculiar to government; it is seen in business, in our social relationship, in religion, in all major human activities. The steps are, perhaps I should say have been, the same and follow in their sequence. There is the long period of indifference and neglect; a period of gradually developing interest; a period of conviction, acceptance and vigorous evangelism, frequently touched off by some accident or dramatic event; a period of consolidation and establishment of these convictions or processes, whatever phase of human interest they represent, into our thinking and practice; and then a gradual falling back to the old order of things — to the old indifference and neglect, only to start the weary round all over again. But this is not so hopeless as it sounds. We level off on a plane higher than the one before and so progress is made — so it must be made. For myself I doubt the short cuts to the millenium.

You will agree, perhaps, that I am not sticking to the text that has been rather wished on me because I haven't said anything about "Consolidating the Gains," but I am coming to that. I have given this little background philosophy in order to try to place more emphasis upon the point that I want to make. The point is this: Government, in the years ahead, I think, is to be the most absorbing and vital interest of the American people, of the world for that matter. It may be that this has always been so. Whatever happens we may expect to see much of the expansion in government that has taken place at the national level continued — and yet greater expansion at the state and local levels; our whole government must be more effective and businesslike in its administration if we are to continue its present form — and possibly its very permanence. It must be well administered by competent people, devoted to the cause of good government, and the resources of the nation must be conserved and developed; the kind of government we must have cannot be attained by incompetency, selfishness and destroying extravagance. Government must be honest and prudent and understanding, or government, our government, must fail.

These things, or notions or facts, are not yet generally clear in the minds of the people. The average citizen may be only dimly conscious of them or may not seem to see them at all. But I admit that these are the factors that make up the background convictions of the people of this country — which have caused them to turn seriously and earnestly to these questions of better public personnel and better personnel practice in government at all of its levels as the foremost problem in the whole field of public administration. These account for the interest in state-wide merit laws in practically every state in the Union and the actual introduction of such laws in a majority of the state legislatures last year.

Whether the cycle theory is true or not, and it would seem to have been generally true, we stand at the high tide of this popular movement — this period of evangelism for the improvement of our whole civil service. We need spend no time speculating on public morals as being at the root of this matter. It is not because we are better or have a keener appreciation of the need for cleansing our governmental service. The conditions that have been long in their development and that have been greatly stimulated by the crises of recent years have compelled this all but universal interest. The time for great advances in the improvement of the performance of the tasks of government — the time of great accomplishment — is here now. This is the time "we long have sought" as the hymn writer says. I confess that I am somewhat overawed by the prospect. We are not well prepared for the tasks that are to be thrust upon us. And if we fail, then the same opportunity will not come again to my generation; it may not come to the generation of those who are just beginning their careers in this field; and no one can tell what the results may be if those who administer government and do its work fail to make our form of government function effectively in the discharge of the tasks and obligations placed upon it.

I say that it is our responsibility — by that, I mean this whole group of those now engaged in public personnel administration, both commissioners, administrators and technicians, and those who have specially prepared themselves to participate in this work — to lead the way in the setting up of public personnel systems and in the administration of public personnel laws in these new state and local governments. I do not say this because I consider the public personnel group as wiser than the rest nor with any feeling of superior devotion or capacity on our part. I know, as you know, how few are the men and women of thought and action in our field. I know, as you know, how many of us falter in our tasks, how we flounder in our techniques, and how too frequently, we fail, in part at least, to do the whole job we undertake. But I know, also, that, contrary to prevailing notions, modern personnel work is a highly specialized kind of service; it requires not only an unusual amount of common sense, capacity and human understanding, but broad knowledge and special techniques. It is no job for amateurs or adventurers. I know also that we represent most of whatever experience and skill there is in the operating field of public personnel administration, and around our knowledge, our practice and our skills and capacity must be built this growing business of public personnel administration.

This is a sobering thought. I wish that I might have the capacity for leadership, or that some one of you might have it, to call for and get the best and all that is in you, and every other man and woman in the country who has the interest and the preparation and the skill, in meeting these challenging responsibilities. But this job is not to be done by the "man on horseback." It must be done by the plodding, determined workers in a thousand places who know their jobs and do them with skill and devotion that will not be denied.

I should like to say to those who have already served through the heat and the toil of the day, that their job is not yet done, that their old zeal and determination, their wisdom and their deepened experience, are demanded now more than ever before. And I should like to say to those who are just entering, or who are about to enter, the field that I envy them for the opportunity for great service that is before them.

Consider, if you will, that there are 175,000 separate governments in these United States, that only 863 of them now have central personnel agencies of any kind, that but 14 states have civil service systems, that central personnel systems will be established, yes, demanded, in literally thousands of these governments within the next ten years, and let your own imagination work.

For fifty years prior to 1935 the annual average increase of new public personnel agencies was about eight. Last year there were thirty or forty new ones, including five states. The propagandists or those engaged in this particular field of civic education seem not to have been convincing. They played their part, a useful one, but the main impetus for this better personnel in government revival came from some other source. Necessity, not repentance, is forcing the issue. It is my notion that this movement will not stop until the personnel director is as familiar as the tax collector. When I think of public budgets, balanced and unbalanced, I think that I can add nothing to the force of that statement.

A great surgeon is supposed to have said once: "If I had but four minutes to perform a vital operation I would take one minute to consider my problem and make my plans." Our doctors tell us too that it is good technique to consider the state of our case and to make some plans.

And what is our situation and outlook? There is a serious shortage of experienced and qualified people in the public personnel field, but there is an increasing amount of talent coming into it and a good supply in the offing. Sixty-one colleges and universities have schools of public administration or place special emphasis on career training in the public service. That was the count last week, I believe. Half of these schools or courses have been instituted within the last five years and three-quarters of them within the last ten years. We are training apprentices in Washington, in the organizations of governmental officials centered in Chicago, and in a number of operating agencies; and in the universities and governmental departments at every level are to be found a great many people of capacity and background who offer promising material for this personnel field. The great problem is not the getting of talent and having it trained and ready ten years from now — I think that we shall have that. We need competent and experienced people now. Both the older agencies and the new are in competition with each other and all of us in seeking trained and experienced people. One-third of our staff has gone within a year, another third would have gone, and every week or two I get widely scattered inquiries seeking experienced personnel. I am satisfied that the experiences of other agencies are about the same. Yet the work in these new agencies must go on. I say that the right kind of public personnel administration or other public work for that matter cannot be done effectively by amateurs. All of the poor jobs in government are not chargeable to the "practical statesmen." There has been entirely too much surveying, classifying, organizing and regulating by amateurs. Crusading zeal is not a substitute for solid experience — and shining eyes are not so dependable as the gray matter that lies behind them.

We shall probably do nothing about all this, but, if I could write the ticket, I would undertake a little directed intelligence on this problem. I would lay the stress on the administrative and operating problems and processes. I would want to draft every able and experienced man or woman from any assignment he or she may now have outside the operating field into this field as quickly as possible. I would let those without practical experience carry the work of education and information as they are able. I would undertake to do the job rather than be content to talk about it. I would urge that the training at college and university level be continued. I would encourage more of the scholarly men and women who know about government to come into the field and learn its actual processes and functioning. I would encourage those already in allied or related public service to acquaint themselves with the problems and the possibilities in the personnel field. And if I had $50,000 a year to spend of other people's money, of course, I would select twenty or twenty-five people, reasonably mature, of broad background training, capable, interested, industrious, and as one of my old cattle friends used to say, "with a loose and mellow hide" and capable of growth, and I would give them directed and intensive training in the problems of personnel administration in civil service commissions and personnel agencies throughout the country, good and bad. In a year or two or three I am satisfied that I would have a crop of younger and new administrators, working like a leaven through the whole public personnel mass. If the public personnel people want an effective program, a plan that will work and bring results, here it is. Interest and energy and cash spent in this way will not only bring big returns now, they are almost certain to turn assured, indeed almost inescapable, mediocrity into an acceptable product, and they might turn possible, yes probable, failure into satisfying success in the most vital part of the whole business of public administration.

Make no mistake, my friends, things are happening in our field. The show is on in the "Big Tent." The elephants are coming, and the undertaker is beckoning to those who can't get in step and keep up with the parade.

CHAPTER 3

Conditions of Reform*

It is not enough merely to indicate what is wrong with the way government in the United States is going about the selection, the training, and the management of its administrative force. Many of those who have written on the subject [1] have not avoided the temptation of trying to make difficult things easy and complicated problems simple. Rarely have the advocates of new procedures for assuring administrative careers recognized that a great deal of *conditioning in public opinion,* as well as in our public service itself, must take place before we may advance with much confidence. The truth of the matter is that there is not yet any recognized administrative class in our governments although there are a great many highly competent men and women in our public service who are fully entitled to be designated as career people.[2] The progress that has been made in the direction of professionalizing the civil service, in providing opportunities for life careers and in developing an administrative class

---

[1] See Sarah Greer, *A Bibliography of Civil Service and Personnel Administration,* Commission of Inquiry on Public Service Personnel, 1935.

[2] For evidence of careers in the public service see Charles P. Messick, "Building Careers in Government," Proceedings, *Forty-First Annual Conference on Government, National Municipal League,* 1935.

* This chapter was originally published as Chapter 9 in Fritz Morstein Marx, ed., *Public Management in the New Democracy* (Harper and Brothers Publishers, New York and London, 1940) pp. 130-142.

has been uneven, costly and without deliberate plan. Public sentiment has acquiesced in this state of affairs without much protest, and certainly without articulate and sustained opposition. And this is perhaps the main reason why there must be wide changes in the attitude of both men in authority and citizens generally before we can get far beyond the conversational stage.

Neither our responsible elective and appointive officials nor the general public have acknowledged the need for a definite administrative service whose members require a special training and educational background and should be selected by methods different from those used in recruiting other civil servants. Government executives, legislators, and departmental officers do not think and act on this theory. Public opinion is not informed and probably not sympathetic to it. This is not to say that we should not work toward the recognition of an administrative class or that skilled administrators are not required. It is only in emphasis of the fact that the ground must be prepared and the foundations put in before we undertake to build the structure itself.

A great deal of lip service has been given recently in support of the application of the merit principle to government personnel at all its levels. This is a hopeful sign but we may not conclude that either in office or as citizens we are ready to renounce all partisanship as it affects our civil service in the use of public employment in reward or in encouragement of political activity. Personnel practices as to the new agencies of the federal government; the quick repeal of the recent civil service legislation in Arkansas; the successful attacks upon the comprehensive personnel system in Michigan, notwithstanding the noble accomplishments of Mr. Brownrigg and his associates in its establishment; similar upheavals in many other places for political reasons — all this is convincing evidence that our public service is not yet free from partisan pressure and domination.

The acceptance of the merit rule in its broad implications must become an accomplished fact. Our civil service must be stabilized. Fitness must be the determining factor both for entrance into and advancement in the service. These are the foundations that are necessary before the framework of a professionalized service [3] and a true career system in public employment can be erected.

When these conditions have been met, the civil service itself must be fully organized in order that the personnel agency may discharge its functions and apply the tools necessary for its use. The service must be *classified* upon the basis of the duties performed and the attaching responsibilities. There must be a comprehensive *compensation* plan providing for reasonable and adequate rates of pay, high enough in the lower brackets to permit public employees to live in accordance with decent standards and sufficient in the higher classes to attract and retain competent people. There must be sound *examination procedure,* an equitable *promotion* system, and a *training* program. There must be opportunity for assignment of promising entrants within and among departments and divisions for training purposes, and the chance of advancing capable people from the ranks. In brief, there must be complete personnel administration, and this should also include service ratings, procedures for the induction of new employees, probation, supervision and discipline, and regulations applying to vacation and sick leave, transfer, layoff, and retirement. All of these essentials are present in a few jurisdictions. In a much greater number of areas we find some of them provided. But in most states and larger municipalities scarcely any of them are part of the routine practice. The United States Civil Service Commission is mostly a testing agency. It neither has the authority nor does it undertake to discharge many of the positive personnel functions so important for the federal service.

---

[3] "Professionalizing the state service does not mean that the State's personnel shall be limited to those belonging to recognized professions, but rather that professional work shall be done by those trained in the professions, that public service shall be looked upon by the government worker as his profession, his business in life, his career, and that in his attitude and work he should be governed by the ethics and industry, the desire for self-improvement and the sense of responsibility that are expected to prevail in professional life." Charles P. Messick, "Professionalizing the State Service," *Annals of the American Academy of Political and Social Science,* Vol. 189, p. 74.

II

In Great Britain there has been deliberate and continued effort to develop the higher administrative service. As a result, the civil service has been set aside as an honored career and its recruitment is closely geared to the educational system. In the United States we have been rather afraid of a select class of civil servants. We have adhered generally to the conception voiced by Andrew Jackson that the work of government could be done by any person of average ability and that anyone who can get into an office is competent to fill it.

In addition to this psychology, peculiar to us as Americans but actually an outgrowth of frontier life in a new country, the imposition of industrial patterns has done much to shape our attitudes. We have assumed that the kind of resourcefulness that has found its way to the top in business is the kind that is needed in government. We have followed the conviction that the business executive can step into government and, without background or training in the ways of public administration, solve all problems and administer successfully any phase of public business. We have overlooked the fact entirely, it seems, that this theory no longer holds in private enterprise and that for a generation or more industry has been sifting out the ablest and best of our university material and training it for executive and administrative positions.

We have tended to follow industry also in our practice of classifying positions in the public service. The foreman or superintendent in industry demands mechanics or operators who can function at once. When he comes over into government he calls for a bookkeeping-machine operator, for instance, who can produce immediate results on the particular type of machine in use or to be purchased. He wants an experienced factory inspector or a motor-vehicle inspector or a health or highway-construction inspector, and employees for literally thousands of other specialties, able to render effective service instantly. Too frequently he loses sight of the fact that our industrial system does not produce many of the specialists needed in the public service. The current policy of narrow specifications in the personnel requests of appointive authorities, reflected as it is in the classification of civil service positions, must be broken down before we can make headway toward the career idea and the establishment of an administrative class.

III

The Commission of Inquiry on Public Service Personnel proposed five general career divisions: [4] (1) The unskilled service; (2) the skilled and trades service; (3) the clerical service; (4) the professional and technical service; and (5) the administrative service. Many who write about the British civil service leave the impression that there is little recruitment for specialized types of service, yet Harvey Walker observed,[5] "There are many hundred classes in the Civil Service." This does not detract, however, from the institutional and organizational significance of Britain's administrative class.

It is probably again our national psychology and our imitation of industry that have induced us to rely on older and more experienced men in our recruitment methods and to prefer specific training to a broad liberal education. The conflicts of opinion as to the respective merits of the British policy of recruiting future administrators at an early age and requiring only high scholarship and a general educational background and the American practice of stressing experience in the selection of men who are to master particular fields will continue, of course, for some time to come. The British prove their system workable by the result obtained and by demonstrating in its operation that it is possible to break through the well-established procedure so as to secure seasoned administrators for the newer services such as traffic, transport, and utilities, when the need is acute. In this country we profess admiration for the British system, but we cling to the notion that we need practical knowledge already acquired rather than potential capacities. Nevertheless, public

---

[4] *Better Government Personnel*, pp. 42ff., 1935.
[5] *Training Public Employees in Great Britain*, p. 6. Commission of Inquiry on Public Service Personnel, 1935.

opinion is turning toward the acceptance of the principles of early recruitment, training, and development of our administrative class. There are a number of jurisdictions having well-defined promotion procedures of this type that are applied in fact, and the movement is gathering momentum and vigor in that direction.

As soon as we begin to consider the problem of recruitment, we come face to face with the old question of the value of a general education as against specific training for specific work. It is difficult to define "an educated person" except in a negative way. It can be said, however, that education may not be measured in years spent in educational institutions, in courses pursued, or in terms of degrees acquired. Educators readily define the untrained mind as one filled with "sketchy, unrelated information," like a "New England attic — a repository of useless and forgotten things."[6] Mr. Roberts defines a trained mind in this way:

> A trained mind is one that has learned through extensive reading of books dealing with several related subjects, as well as through the guidance of competent teachers, to understand why the subjects are related; to criticize intelligently the statements and opinions that it encounters in its reading; to distinguish between that which is false and worthless and that which is genuine and worthy; to think, in short, for itself, and to go on thinking for itself through life; to speak and write clearly and logically on any subject concerning which it has formed an opinion; and to have a sincere appreciation of and respect for intellectual pursuits.[7]

There is force to the argument that our institutions of higher learning should train minds rather than training individuals in special techniques presumably valuable in particular trades or businesses. It is sounder procedure to delay specialization until there is substantial general training. We may profess it, but actually do not put into practice the theory that general training is all that is required and that the mind that is truly trained can "master any trade or business in a few months, or a few weeks, if not in a few days." Notwithstanding the fact that

---

[6] Kenneth Roberts, "Murmuring Michigan," *The Saturday Evening Post*, March 31, 1934, p. 10.

[7] *Ibid.*

a great many American colleges and universities have established schools of public administration and are coming more and more to emphasize the importance of training in this field, fortunately they have not abandoned the notion that the university's obligation is to prepare the student for life rather than to attempt to equip him for some particular public service he may never undertake.[8]

IV

Whatever the advantages of the British system in favor of a broad educational background, it would seem clear that it is not the final answer to our own public service recruiting problems. There is at least some criticism in England of the composition of the administrative class, for a large proportion of its members come from the upper classes. This criticism rests on the feeling that a great proportion should have the life experience and background common to a larger section of the population. The average American is not likely to be convinced that competence is limited to the "educated classes" or that high educational qualifications should be maintained as flat prerequisites. In the United States it would seem likely that recruiting methods for the administrative class will fall somewhere between the British concept of "testing for the service" and the American practice of "testing for the job."

This will mean for us a certain degree of modification. Indeed, it is interesting to note the number and variety of the widely scattered efforts at each level of government in the United States today to professionalize the government service, to bring prospective career personnel into it, and to develop them into administrators. The experience of the United States Civil Service Commission in recruiting college graduates by means of general tests for junior civil service examiner in 1934 and again in subsequent years is highly pertinent.[9]

---

[8] See Report of the University of Wisconsin's Committee in *Training for Municipal Administration*, International City Managers' Association, 1936, pp. 10 ff.

[9] See Leonard D. White, *Government Careers for College Graduates*, Civil Service Assembly, 1937.

The California State Personnel Board, the New Jersey State Civil Service Commission and the Los Angeles County Civil Service Commission have carried on a similar policy of recruitment for more than 10 years. A number of other public personnel departments have initiated similar undertakings. An examination of the "class specifications" fixed for the tests given by these agencies indicates the emphasis placed upon general education. The test announcements show that full college or university training is required, and that the tests are not limited to those majoring in public administration but are open to graduates who have maintained acceptable standards of scholarship and who have majored in other subjects.

The tests themselves are designed to measure the broad knowledge and capacity of the applicant and not to determine his special training in a particular field. The weakness in our procedure under these tests as compared with the British test for assistant principal, for instance, would seem to be the failure to connect up our recruitment processes with our educational system, the method of open competition followed, appointment in the order of individual standing from the resulting eligible lists, lack of strict adherence to the scholastic type of examination and the use of unstandardized tests; and probably the level of difficulty and the content of the examination itself. The encouraging factor is the indication that there is increasing support for professionalizing our civil service, for increasing its prestige, and for the conscious development of career opportunities.

It is worthwhile also to inquire into the results flowing from the efforts to recruit on the basis of general education. The innovations of the United States Civil Service Commission are too recent to permit relevant appraisal. While they may not have been entirely successful and may require further refinement, as Dr. White indicates,[10] they did bring into the federal service several hundreds of college graduates who survived the keenest kind of competition and who are decidedly above average capacity.

The present director of the California State Personnel Board entered the service by way of the same recruiting policy.

----

[10] *Ibid.*

The assistant director and the senior staff member of the Civil Service Assembly came into the public personnel field through identical methods and received their initial training in the New Jersey system. And scattered throughout the state, local, and the federal services are many who were selected through general tests, who display the professional attitude toward their work, and who are finding places as public administrators.

V

In training, whether pre-entry or post-entry, there are the same uncertainty and varying practices as are found in recruitment. The outstanding characteristic, however, is the almost universal interest in the subject shown by educators, by institutions of higher learning, by a rapidly increasing number of public officials, by a wide variety of civic organizations, and by a large body of citizens. There are about seventy-five schools and departments of public administration in our colleges and universities. The number grows almost month by month. The National Institute of Public Affairs in Washington and the School of Citizenship and Public Affairs at Syracuse University are good examples of organized pre-entry training. The most ambitious program of post-entry training undertaken by any college or university, perhaps, is that of the American University at Washington. The training activities of the United States Department of Agriculture have extended over a long period and may well be considered the forerunner of the program organized by the American University. In addition, similar programs exist in several of the federal departments and agencies that contribute materially to the preparation of federal employees for the professional and administrative service.

It must be remembered, however, that not all of the career-service training is carried on at the federal level. The same tendencies are present in the state and local government services. Hundreds of training projects, from an informal internship arrangement in a small department or division to the full-fledged police or fire training schools, are operated in practically all parts of the country. The training programs of the University of California at Berkeley and of the University of Southern California, representative of this category, have been conducted successfully for a number of years. The International City Managers' Association, the Municipal Finance Officers' Association and the Civil Service Assembly have not only encouraged the organization and extension of such training programs, but have contributed to their realization by assistance in the formulation of courses and the creation of a limited number of internships in their respective fields.

It is hence not fair to say that the United States has failed either in its understanding of the importance or in the actual initiation of a training program for its civil servants. It would seem that the conditions here are about the same as in many other governmental undertakings. We have not thought the problems through. There is still an almost complete lack of long-range planning in the training field, although headway is being made and we are becoming increasingly aware of the problems involved.

VI

The obstacles to and the progress of reform in both recruitment and training of an administrative class have been outlined in the preceding pages. The present state of our thinking and practice in this field would seem to add up about as follows:

(1) Successful public administration in the United States requires at all levels of government a competent civil service and a high degree of administrative skill.

(2) There is as yet no recognized administrative class in the American public service and there have been only scattered efforts to recruit potential administrators.

(3) The American method has been to recruit as administrators men of experience from business and professional schools or depend upon the accidental discovery of administrative talent within the service itself.

(4) Since American governmental undertakings have expanded so rapidly in recent years, it is being generally recognized that a resourceful and stable civil service is essential to good administration, that government should attract and retain a fair share of the best products of our educational system, and that administrative talent must be sought and cultivated.

(5) An adequate recruitment procedure for the administrative class depends upon accepted conditions and settled convictions with respect to our civil service. This procedure must grow out of our attitude and the recognition of our needs. It cannot be formulated upon a predetermined plan.

(6) University training should be for life rather than for narrow civil service specialization because the public employment field is limited and there is no assured procedure for bringing aspirants so trained into the service in steady volume.

(7) For some years to come the American people are likely to continue the practice of bringing into government administrators from business and the professions rather than adopting a policy of training all or nearly all of the administrative class within the service.

(8) The policy actually to emerge is likely to be a compromise between the notion that administrators learn only by experience in business and professional fields and must hence be recruited from these sources and the European conception that the administrative class should be brought into the public service directly from the universities and trained in the service.

(9) Post-entry training will soon become a widely accepted part of our public personnel administration. The objectives should be clearly determined and methods developed without delay.

(10) Recruitment methods for the administrative class must be expected to continue to be uncertain for the time being, but valid procedures should be developed as rapidly as possible. One of the essential steps is the modification of our highly specialized classification system so as to provide much fewer and more general classes.

CHAPTER 4

The Merit System in New Jersey

The place and the part of the merit system in government was established to a greater extent in New Jersey than anywhere else in the nation. It is with a great deal of satisfaction that I am able to make this statement and claim the leadership.

"Mr. Civil Service"

I joined the New Jersey State Civil Service Commission as a special examiner in 1910, served as assistant chief examiner of the Commission from 1912 to 1917, and then as the Commission's chief examiner and secretary from 1917 to 1949. We took our responsibility seriously. We worked hard. We stuck to our guns. We made progress. As the executive officer of the Commission, I bore the brunt of the administrative work. In time, many people called me "Mr. Civil Service," both in New Jersey and throughout the country.

I do not claim to deserve such a significant title, but I must admit that by reason of our work and accomplishments in New Jersey, we gained attention at home and throughout the nation. As I became more and more the voice of the Commission, I received most of the credit. But it happened that the public gave me the credit, and what I accomplished was by reason of the permission and approval of the Commission.

Early Training

I have been involved in many varied projects throughout my lifetime. My training was limited. A farm boy who learned to work, I attended a little one-room country school with one teacher who was trained in a similar little school.

I never went to high school. The first day I ever spent in a high school was later when I was a teacher in a high school. Accordingly, I was not qualified for college, but I was admitted nevertheless to Delaware College, now the great University of Delaware. I studied there as I worked on the farm, long days and nights, and first my classmates and then the student body accepted my leadership. I was chairman of the student body, the top officer in command of what we would now call the ROTC, captain of the football team, and president of my class — which office I yet hold. I graduated at the head of my class with a pretty good record.

In 1907, the year I graduated from college, there was a depression, and jobs were hard to find. Even our best engineering graduates felt themselves lucky to find a job where they could earn $15 a week. I concluded quickly that I must continue my education if I were to become recognized among college men. I continued my education, therefore, and was awarded a Master's degree at Delaware College in 1909 and another at the University of Pennsylvania in 1911.

A few years later, when I was promoted to my first executive job in the Civil Service, I had completed 21 of the 24 counts needed for a Ph.D. at the University of Pennsylvania. I had selected the subject of my doctoral dissertation and had collected most of the data upon which it was based. But with all the things I was trying to do at the time, I was obliged to give up my graduate work.

The Need for Change

Along the way of my busy life, I planned to enter the legal profession, but by accident, I began part-time service with the

Civil Service Commission of New Jersey in 1909. I entered Civil Service employment as an assistant examiner in 1910, and was appointed as the Commission's executive officer in 1917. While I was disappointed at first in not following the profession I had hoped to follow, I do have a feeling of satisfaction that I have made some contribution to the ongoing movement for better government.

In 1908, the first New Jersey Civil Service Law was enacted. Boss leadership had reached a high point in New Jersey, and as happened then and yet happens, protest and opposition resulted. Such was and is the process — the people vote the bosses out and a change for the better appears to occur. Unfortunately, time shows that the change becomes old and neglected, and the government is taken over by the bosses and the old regime begins again. I have seen this happen more than once in my long life.

We take great pride in America that the people rule and that that type of government is good government and can be made to continue for a long period. But bossism became dominant again and again, and thus became destructive. A constructive ending to the story would be to say that bossism has been eradicated, but that result has not occurred in any state or in any level of government, including the government in Washington.

One of the main achievements of that time was the limiting of the appointive power of the authorities within the system. Their attitude was, as it still is, negative. Those in power felt, and some still feel, that the merit system is all right for "them," but not for "us." In the earlier part of this century, the response to such new ideas, among those who felt curtailed by the merit system, was more violent and much less subtle than it is today.

There is no reason for discouragement in the fact that we as individuals or as a whole have not reached perfection. That is only a goal in the distance. Improvement is what we seek, not revolution. The merit system now has spread to practically every public jurisdiction, department, district, municipality, county, and township in the states and the nation.

As the merit system took root, sprouted, and thrived, I tried always to set an example of hard work and fair dealing. In this way we were able to stay ahead of the crowd. My colleagues and I built on good will. My staff was small but strong, and willing to work hard; an example I tried almost beyond reason to set.

Devotion

Among public employees, generally, within the early part of this century, I do not hesitate to say there was a greater devotion to work, and more appreciation by them for their protections and opportunities, than existed later. They appeared, too, to have had better qualifications and dedication, and more personal interest in their work and in their agencies and departments. This was true because of the chastening effects of the war years — of 1917 and 1918. We were glad to have peace and the opportunity to rebuild the strength and the confidence we had before, and this attitude extended throughout our whole society — including politicians, departmental authorities, and the public.

We in New Jersey were prepared for this projected change. Thinking and action turned to harmonious pursuits, as business and industry were anxious to return to normal activity and profit. And government was equally eager to revert to constructive enterprise. The people had believed that World War I was "the war to end all wars," and that belief spurred their postwar energies toward a renewal of the former constructive patterns of growth.

With such labor and devotion, we — as well as other jurisdictions — had saved the form and fabric of the merit system. I believe it can be said that New Jersey led most of the states in pulling flesh back on the bones. It was necessity rather than virtue, however, that compelled our attitude and our action.

Opposition

Notwithstanding the return of peace, there was almost as much opposition to the merit system, it seemed to us, as at its inception. In 1919, after having passed through the destructive World War, the country was trying to get back to a peace basis.

This meant, of course, sudden and drastic changes throughout government and our whole economic system. During the war period, every normal peacetime activity had been urged to cease. Departmental heads were permitted to appoint staff as they deemed necessary and to pay what they wished. Many of these demands were forestalled, due to our diligence. I am obliged to say that the responsibility for maintaining the principles and practice of an active merit system fell upon me. Many times, I was much alone. Although some of the commissioners were half-convinced that surrender of the merit system was imminent, they did agree that I should stick to my guns. With help mustered from the employee associations and more conservative department heads, we were able to keep the merit system intact.

No matter how well the work of the personnel agency is done, the old notion that "to the victor belongs the spoils" still lurks in the minds of many of our governing authorities. They yet want to make their own selection of their own employees as they did before the civil service system was instituted. They want to select their own people to do the work that they are expected to do and have the responsibility for having done their work honestly, properly and well. That is natural. As I write this, in the year 1977, we see the same policy in action not only at the local and state levels, but reaching to the highest officials in the land. No matter what is said officially, the policy lingers on.

Service to Governors and Commissioners

I think that it may be said that our success with the merit system spread in great measure into many areas throughout the nation. We worked for and with the various governors of the state of New Jersey, and with the legislative committees, particularly those on appropriations and personnel matters. They knew our plans, that we were trying to help and that their efforts were made easier by our own successes in the management of the civil service system. Each year, as budget-making time approached, we were able to furnish detailed and intelligent data regarding plans for what needed to be done, and inventories of the wants and needs of each department. This type of assistance determined and forged the policies of personnel management throughout the state.

A continuing and helpful, as well as a cordial, relationship was developed with both houses of the legislature. We sent qualified clerks and stenographers to the legislature, to assist in their individual and committee work, which theretofore had been unknown to them. The system was a success because it was economical and sensible. It introduced new ways of cooperation and information by an agency that knew more about the actual needs of the departmental divisions than budget officers knew, and an agency that was willing to help at all times. This was something new in our state at least; that system prevails to this day.

I agree that my own activities, during the period I was a civil servant, extended beyond that expected of any single officer. Personally, I rendered many, many services to governors, senators, assemblymen, and committee members through the years. I became in service an assistant to the governors without portfolio and had a constructive influence in the state business. I wrote for governors. I acted as consultant to many legislative committees and wrote their reports. As an example, I wrote the relief plan for the city of Trenton in 1932. I wrote the statewide relief act for the Governor almost the next day. I rewrote the Civil Service Rules and the proposed Civil Service Statute in 1929 and 1930. Indeed, I am charged with having written more New Jersey state papers than any other person, living or dead.

This type of work lays one open to many personal risks as administrations change. But I served in the office I held longer than any other person in such an office — from 1917 to 1949 — in the nation's history. When I retired, voluntarily and on my own action, I was able to say also that no civil service commissioner I worked with during that period left office without being my friend and supportive of me. There were times, of course, when it was difficult for commissioners — as other public officers — to know or to do the thing that should be done in the public interest. I did and said what I thought was the correct thing and assumed the responsibility therefor. I strove to initiate, to teach, to guide. I have no control of what others do. I can and have made mistakes. I claim no merit in what I did. I tried merely to be myself.

I have already commented enough about the many things that make up the administration of the personnel agency. I have not covered the field here. In spite of the risk of raising in the minds of those who may read these lines the impression that I am an admirer of myself, which I am not, I am led to further discussion of other problems. In fact, in personnel work, public or private, one touches almost every factor that makes up the working life of people. This section, more than any other in this book, takes on the nature of a diary, where one man writes his own story of a work, in which he was in some measure successful for the possible benefit of others.

The Governor's Study Commission

Another attack on the merit system came from a body called the Governor's Study Commission, created to overrule the Civil Service Commission. Specifically, the Study Commission proposed that the testing of applicants for public service should be taken out of the hands of the Director of the present Civil Service Commission and left to the appointing authority. To do this would destroy the whole merit system. I am against any other agency that stands between the Civil Service department and the appointment authorities or the appointees. I believe that public service employment, with the pay levels and increasing fringe benefits attached, will again become much sought after, that true competitive testing will return, and that the real advantages of a proper handling of personnel matters will accrue to the state as well as to the general public. There is no doubt in my mind that the merit system, properly manned and properly applied, insures better public administration and, in addition, saves money.

Post World War I

Raises in pay had been delayed during World War I, and, therefore, after the war both employees and departmental authorities were anxious for immediate relief. In the name of the Commission, I checked the appropriations' balances in all state departments and agencies. I found that many of the departments, as the budget period neared its end, played the old game of transferring funds from one account to another where they could be spent. Otherwise, the up-coming appropriation committee review would discover them and become stubborn about increases the following year. As all experienced executives, supervisors, and directors know, this is an old game that is yet popular and is yet working.

At that time, I advocated a clever method of redistributing the balances. I found that with these balances we could give a fairly good raise in pay without asking any special appropriations. I explained the situation to my Commission, and with its approval I went to the Governor who also gave his approval. By pooling all departmental balances, a bonus payment for all state employees was planned. I prepared detailed regulations, setting forth the condition and amounts that should be allocated to each class and employee. We held a departmental conference. The unbelievers were not convinced, but they approved the plan. The legislature adopted it. The distribution of these wayward funds turned out to be more difficult than the finding of them, and the doubters, as usual, were most difficult to satisfy, but it turned out to be a rewarding coup for most everyone concerned.

Close on the heels of this experience, the returning veterans asked for jobs in the public service without examination and without reference to their qualifications. Both sentiment and need were attached to this request, but had this plan been accepted, it would have set back the merit system and the Civil Service Commission's work indefinitely, and the building of to that date would have been destroyed.

A compromise was worked out. The Chairman of the Commission proposed a plan that I prepared. The plan warded off the proposal that returning veterans alone should be given all public peacetime employment without examination as to fitness or other qualifications. Sympathy was on their side. It was difficult for me to oppose it, especially as I had not been called to active service because of my age and the public work I was doing.

Our plan called for giving certain credit points for overseas veterans, and placing those who passed the regular tests in line for early appointments. This helped the veterans, and saved the basic part of the merit system.

Advancement of the Merit System

In 1913, I met E. O. Griffenhagen of Chicago. He was ahead of all others in his conception of the quality of the public service. We became friends at once. He is yet alive, but he retired some years ago and seemingly takes no interest in any outside matters. He was the one man in America most involved in the inception and formulation of the classification of jobs in this country. In retrospect, what he accomplished appears simple, but it was at the time an important discovery or invention, as are many innovations couched in common sense.

He noted that there were some positions that were similar in duties and difficulty, which could be classed together for testing, pay, and other purposes, while there were others sufficiently different to be put in other groups or left standing alone. He hit upon the word "class" to simplify the problems involved. The Chinese had done something similar thousands of years ago, and New Zealand had such a system in part, at least. But we in America did not know of their advancements at this time. It may now seem to be a simple thing, but it was a dedicated advance in the whole selective procedure, and remains the foundation of our civil service system today.

My acquaintance with Griffenhagen in 1913 began a lifelong friendship of benefit to both of us, and to the system of personnel administration with which both of us have been connected. I too, have retired, but I am still beating the drums of interest in, and talking and writing about, personnel management in the public service. I worked with Griffenhagen at times for the Canadian government in a comprehensive study of the government organization and personnel of Canada, the first and largest undertaking of its kind, and incidentally the most successful one, ever attempted in the Americas. Wide reorganizational changes were proposed, most of which were accepted and implemented.

During this study, I met Fred Telford, a member of Griffenhagen's staff. Telford was an able man, restless and full of ideas, but always in a hurry. From that time onward, Telford worked with or for me, and he, too, made his contribution to the personnel management that we have today. To Griffenhagen's classifications, Telford added descriptions of duties and proposed qualification requirements. He thus completed the job specifications and my refinements. Testing them brought acceptance, and they are yet used today with but minor modifications.

Telford's contribution to the advancement of personnel administration has been exceedingly important and equal to that of any other person in the field. I hesitate to claim importance for my own contribution even today, but in frankness I am constrained to say that Griffenhagen, Telford and I constituted the leaders of public personnel management and administration in America.

A Turning Point

I do not deny my part in the improvement in public administration. In 1919 and 1920, the public service in New Jersey and the nation had come to a place in its development where the public wanted to hear about the development of the civil service system. At the annual meeting of the Assembly of Civil Service Commissioners in Rochester in 1919, I was asked to tell something of our work in personnel management. I rarely speak of this portion of the civil service story, but it was a turning point in my developing policies and represented another step forward.

At an informal conference before the official opening of the meeting, fifteen or twenty of the older leaders, nearly all of them commissioners, met for an informal discussion of their problems. One of the number, who had had a longer and wider experience than the others, chaired the discussion. He opened the meeting, outlined the reasons for it, and spoke about some of his own problems in New York. Then one after another, all of the commissioners spoke in the same vein. Their stories were similar. They were having trouble; they might lose their jobs; things were bad in general. They all told a dreary story. The longer they talked, the more uncomfortable I became. The chairman broke in finally to say: "Yes, we are not doing well, not as well as we know how to do, but if we should do as well as we know how to do we would lose our jobs." At that point I blurted out with more disappointment than diplomacy, saying:

> I have not had the experience that you men have had, but I have been at it long enough to be convinced that the things we are trying to do are of vital importance to our governments. I think they are more important than you or me. You say that you do not do as well as you know how to do. If that is the way you feel, I think it might not be too bad if some of you did lose your jobs.

As I sat down, I wondered what would happen next. My remarks about ended the meeting, and to my surprise and relief nearly all of them gathered around me and began commending me for talking back. Apparently, they had a new leader, because they asked me: "What shall we do?" I admit that I was somewhat nervous, but I tried hard to keep my cool. I was able to respond: "I don't know much about how or what we can do next, but there are foundations — the Rockefeller Foundation, for example — that offer funds for research and study of various kinds on what they consider important. I suggest you appoint a committee to go into the matter and see what we can find out and what if anything we can do."

A committee was appointed, I was designated chairman, and we were in business. Two years later, then as President of the Assembly of Civil Service Commissioners, I was able to report to the annual meeting that we had been granted a study fund that would be continued for some years if the Assembly as a body approved our efforts. I had been accorded some recognition for my work theretofore in New Jersey, but now my national leadership role was on its way.

Under the study grant, the Bureau of Public Personnel was established under the aegis of the Institute of Government in Washington. I was named to represent the civil service system.

Fred Telford was made secretary of the organization, and together we went to work.

The Bureau continued for ten years. Telford traveled over the country, carrying encouragement and technical aid to personnel agencies everywhere. I stayed in New Jersey working out what I considered the place and the part of the personnel agency in government. By the middle of the 1920's I thought I had something to say, and that it was time to talk about it.

Civil Service Assembly: 1926

I could very well stop here, and I suspect that I have used "I" more than "we." But in this last writing, I am merely trying to tell the story of my own activities in a long life of public service, not as a matter of vanity, but in the hope that my story will encourage those who come after me to do their best in whatever roles they assume.

At the 1926 meeting of the Civil Service Assembly, I said that, among other advancing practices, it was time to recognize the fact that the personnel agency, to do its job, must be an integral part of the government. The practice of the personnel agency handing its rulings and actions over the barrier, or under it, or around it, always on the outside of things, must be ended. This is what had come about in New Jersey.

Proceeding further, I said that government required, and must have enough, qualified employees to do the work of government that needed to be done, and no more, that they should be properly organized, properly supervised, adequately but not extravagantly paid, and fairly treated for doing a fair day's work, every workday. I should say here, and most people believe, that our governments are wasteful in many ways, and one of the wastes in government is the keeping of agencies to do things just because they have done them before, with no heed to the real needs. Of course, they should be abolished. This philosophy that I then expressed became a part of the philosophy and ideals of public personnel management that have been adopted in principle by most government jurisdictions in the United States.

Nevertheless, it is always difficult to get the work of government properly done and to assure that positive action is taken. That must come about eventually — a task for the future.

New Commission, New Law: 1929

Just as the old grow weak and fail in their duties, so also did the old Civil Service Commission in New Jersey become weak and indifferent. Accordingly, in 1929 the old Commission was removed from office by the Governor, and a new Commission was appointed. It had been reported that some employees in some jurisdictions were not being certified by the personnel department before receiving payment. A legislative committee was appointed; our staff was directed to investigate and furnish the data to that committee. This was done. The Commission had not done well in handling themselves, either individually or collectively. They were therefore removed from office. The offenses were not of great consequence, but they were illegal. It became my duty to acquaint the new Commission members with their duties, an obligation I had undertaken throughout my experience as a public servant. I followed with that Commission the same course I had followed from the beginning. I reported every important action of each meeting and each succeeding meeting, explaining the legalities as I saw them, outlining the necessary legislation, delineating the probable difficulties as they might arise. I always prepared the annual and other reports and public announcements made by the Commission as a body or by individual Commissioners.

Around that time, a new law needed to be written. The existing laws were a mass of amendments and additions to the original statute. I wrote a new law in plainest words, omitting redundancy, i.e., the old "provided"s and "however"s. Aside from the matter of pay in local governments, this new revision was adopted almost word for word as written. It was an important landmark, gained with some appeasement of the new Commission. It contained the authority intended, with the amendments necessary to assure passage.

The chief difference between the old law and the new was clarity. The old law was a compilation of provisions of the Federal law, the New York State and City laws, the Commonwealth of Massachusetts law, plus some original stipulations designed to fit New Jersey's own situation. The old law, originally written by an assistant attorney general and an able lawyer, had been amended so many times that it was almost impossible to find two attorneys in agreement as to its interpretation. The new law was intended to be clear and definite in its meaning.

Many persons and organizations have formulated model laws, but most of their authors have not had to stand, as I did, on the firing line, simultaneously trying to run a large and complicated merit system while being challenged regarding the results and merits of that system.

Developing Problems

Efficiency and economy are major factors to be considered in business, industry, and government. Awareness of such needs brought about the emergence of professional efficiency engineers. Some of them were neither engineers nor efficient, but they were on the right track; they rendered good service. Then came the sociologists to fit the round pegs into the round holes, and the square pegs into the square holes. Their advances and discoveries have not been neglected. Next came the teams that found "the one best way to do things," with the "cheaper by the dozen" family group, usually containing at least one able family member.

I remember Robert Hutchins, the boy wonder of Harvard, the young President of the University of Chicago. He laid down some significant groundwork, with good ideas for the improvement of the University of Chicago. I watched closely the benefits gained by him for his faculty, in the midst of certain amounts of rancor. The brilliance of this man led him to the leadership of a self-perpetuating group that deliberated the destiny of mankind. From the nation's leading universities came educators and social scientists to help governments deal with their management problems.

The economists and psychologists must be included among these experts. It has always seemed to me that the economists have lost a first-rate opportunity to put their stamp on government. They should have had a much greater influence on government than they have had. The psychologists, on the other hand, have supplied the testing field with valuable assistance. They reminded us that big things are made up of a lot of little things, and that to gain understanding we must turn to the little things. They gave us the short-answer tests, which are used everywhere for intelligence measurement and many other purposes.

Now we find individuals and firms everywhere who offer expertise in any line and for any purpose one can think of. Almost every government, big and little, hires one or more of these people or firms to do special studies whenever action is desired in any area considered important by the governing body. At the moment, New Jersey has the fever. I recall doing those jobs within my departments myself, doing them better just because we knew our territory and our people. As a matter of fact, I created one of these management consulting companies myself after my retirement in 1949.

Testing is one of the major factors in the system. I had been a student and teacher for a number of years before I entered the personnel field, so I was familiar with the writing and scoring of tests. The civil service reformers proposed to use written tests to select qualified public employees. We yet use them, but they are not enough. A number of examiners in the field began to realize that a test should relate to the duties and responsibilities of the job, as well as to the qualifications required for the job. Simple common sense was coming to the fore.

Most personnel people include an oral interview as a portion of all tests in cases where the duties of an appointee would involve contact with the public. This part of the test can be abused, but I have always stood by it and I used it regardless of that possible abuse. My test was, and would be yet were I still active, divided into at least four parts: (1) education, training and experience; (2) duties; (3) physical and medical standards, where they pertained; and (4) oral interview.

As mentioned earlier, the psychologists have helped the system with their innovations in testing. The civil service field has made wide use of the short-answer tests, both for the intelligence quotients and for some of the job groups. However, these are time-consuming, difficult to prepare, and difficult to validate. Measuring the results, it was found that the ratings obtained were supposed to rise like a pyramid with a broad base in a somewhat straight and diminishing line to a rounded top, and to descend the other side in the reverse of the ascending line. We are all familiar with the "curving" of grades in the academic world.

A member of my staff used quantities of these results, from police and prison officer tests, as the basis for his doctoral dissertation. When I asked him about the significance of his research, and its application to the determination of cut-off points between eligibles and failures, he was unable to respond. I have not yet found acceptable answers to those very questions, but the gentleman who studied this material nevertheless served a long and useful career in public personnel work and as a university professor.

Merit ratings of employees in New Jersey were established early in my time as a part of promotion examinations. J. B. Probst, the Secretary and Examiner of the city of St. Paul, devised a complicated form in the thirties, and I wrote a foreword for the pamphlet approving the plan. Mr. Probst made the mistake of throwing an air of mystery about it. He kept the rating key to himself. It is unfortunate he did not explain his plan to others. Nevertheless, I believe that it represented a constructive move toward this important but difficult problem in recording relative value of employees.

The farther we go into the internals of the merit system, the more we find that training must be taken into consideration by those whose duty is to use and direct it. I had worked out the procedures before others, and without much forethought or planning. My office became the training school for administrators and technicians for other personnel agencies. In this manner, our influence spread to other states, and members of my staff went to Michigan, Connecticut, New York, Louisiana, Tennessee, and elsewhere. It is not too much to say, and I take satisfaction in being able to say so, that the New Jersey system significantly influenced personnel practice throughout the nation.

The Princeton Surveys

Princeton University was in the state of New Jersey, but not of it. It was highly respected, and it was considered a privilege by college students to be admitted. Mr. Frank D. Schroth, Assistant Publisher of the Times Newspapers, suggested that Professor Harold Dodds of Princeton University make a study of the Trenton government. Dodds' long-time interest in public affairs was widely known. His report was followed by a study of the Mercer County government.

By reason of some happenings in some of the state departments, there developed a feeling that a study should be made of the state government. I was asked by some of the legislators what I thought about it, and who should do the job. I indicated my favor of the proposal, and suggested Dr. Dodds. Assisted by a number of younger men, Dr. Dodds undertook the task and made our office their state headquarters. Some improper practices were discovered, and a few people lost their jobs. The study was done well and had a wholesome effect. After Dr. Dodds became President of Princeton, he was obliged to give up all other outside service. Nevertheless, he set up the Princeton Surveys as a permanent organization to study government at state and local levels. He was particularly fortunate in recruiting Dr. John Sly as Director. I had known Dr. Sly from earlier associations at the Institute of Government at the University of Virginia. I kept in close touch with the Surveys as long as they existed. They performed a useful service.

Pledge of Faith and Service

Back in the 1930's and 1940's, I could see that employees needed a greater voice in what was being done in departmental activities as well as in actions affecting them. This became more apparent as my active service in the system drew to a close. The employees had no written statement of their belonging. As a step in that direction, I wrote and circulated a code of conduct among the service, which was widely distributed throughout the country.

Entitled "The Civil Servant's Pledge of Faith and Service," it was written as follows:

> I have faith in my country and its institutions. I believe in the importance of my job and in the dignity of all public service. I count myself fortunate to live and work in a state where I may obtain public employment through competition fairly won under a system which permits me to look forward to a career as a public employee, and to advancement through merit.

> I know that government is no better than the people who direct its affairs and do its work. I will be honest, loyal, and industrious in the work I have to do. I will be courteous in my relations with my superiors, my fellow workers, and the public. I will use public property entrusted to my care for the purposes intended, and protect and conserve it as though it were my own.

> I will refrain from doing anything that will bring discredit upon the state as my employer or upon me as a civil servant. I will strive, through my acts and my work, to realize the purposes for which government is established and so merit the esteem and respect of the people.

This was the first known effort to put into words what might be considered the attitude of the faithful and devoted public employees. Since then, millions of hours and dollars have been devoted to codes of conduct in hundreds of organizations of all kinds. Committees and individuals in the public personnel field have spent a very great deal of time formulating such statements, and there are several versions of such codes. I am a little prejudiced in this matter, I admit, but I prefer the one I wrote in one afternoon. It is an interesting pastime to compare these various versions. My code is yet used, as far as I know, in some parts of the nation. It has the distinction of being the first effort to give to the workers a sense of participation in the maintenance and extension of the merit system, its process, meaning, and purpose.

The End of the 1930's

The state of the merit system in New Jersey at the end of the 1930's was seriously affected by the dangers of those troubled times, as was everybody in our nation. We struggled to continue on the broad foundations we had built, but there were some changes. The laws and powers of the chairman of my Commission were extended. Before he had become fully informed, he was persuaded to give up much of the controlling authority that we had built up. The authority of personnel management has been changed too many times. It yet remains, but without being too critical I must say that it is not as effective as it had been.

Labor-management relations were not usually difficult. Employees were getting bolder, and more so-called leaders were beginning to talk about their rights. To my mind, they have gone much too far and beyond their proper place. But we have these organizations among us, and some solution must be found and agreed to that will maintain the standards and relationships that there must be between the public workers and their supervisors. The public business must go on.

The system of the unionization of public employees has now been extended to much of the nation's public service.

The 1940's and World War II

Moving along through the years now, the Second World War came and went, and its effects were about as distressing and upsetting as those of the First World War had been. It is hardly necessary to say that state and local government cannot operate normally in time of war.

The 1940's affected the merit system in several ways in New Jersey. New Jersey's new Constitution, for example, weakened rather than strengthened the merit system procedures, although it did decidedly improve many parts of the public service.

The enactment of legislation that raised the Chairman — the President of the Commission — to a higher status and clothed him with new and extensive powers was a very important piece of legislation. No longer was this position subject to Commission ruling or decision; rather its incumbent became an agent of the Governor. While I was in service these expanded powers were not wisely handled. Yet our experience and our demonstration showed the possibilities of a well-established system.

Civil Service Hearings

Notwithstanding my own efforts to make hearings for civil service employees investigational rather than court-like hearings, we yet had what in essence were formal hearings, and there seemed to be little reason that they should have been changed.

The old adage, "Justice delayed is justice denied," is one of the eternal verities of our restless world. In the present system, some cases run on for years, because of the act of an improper employee or that of an impetuous departmental authority. Such delays are disturbing to the victim, bad for the individual and department involved, wasteful of unwarranted expense to department, government, and public alike. This is no way to maintain effective administration. Any ordinary appeal, so far as the personnel department is concerned, can and should be settled in thirty days. I repeat: the personnel department is not a court. If there must be a court trial, the aggrieved party should go to the courts in the first instance.

The Right to Strike

I believe in the organization of public employees. I still carry a membership card in the New Jersey State Employees Association. I was a member of the first group of state employees that met secretly in a downtown office in Trenton. The men worked unselfishly for the observance of the civil service laws and the proper protection of public employees. I do not believe, however, that public employees should have the right to strike. It is not that the government's handling of public employees' interests and appeals have always been right and equitable, but our public employees are now given more consideration than that given by any other country or government in the world.

I believe firmly that, with all its faults and failures, our form of government is the best for this nation and for all Americans. Hence, no employee should refuse to perform the duties assigned to him and for which he is employed. I have been, for most of a century, devoted to the cause of the civil service system. If I had had a grievance that could not be adjusted to my satisfaction, I would have resigned. I would not strike against my government. Besides, it is elemental to me that only governing legislative bodies can bargain away monies for which appropriations have not already been made.

I do not ask that anyone accept my conclusions in this matter. I recommend looking into the history books to find what happened to governments that could not or would not enforce their own laws, rules, and regulations. They did not endure.

Some have claimed that, without the right to strike, public employees are second-class citizens. I have spent most of my working life as a public servant. I have always considered myself to be a privileged citizen. I worked in a position that offered an opportunity to serve in the improvement of the operation and functioning of every citizen's government. I encouraged other governmental jurisdictions to follow the example of the civil service system.

I recall at one time that a laboring group in Newark, New Jersey, went on strike. The group included waste collectors. There were charges and counter-charges, as usual. The Civil Service Commission stood firm and did not support the strike. We set an example for the public service that lasted for many years. Such an approach should be revived.

Some Current Thoughts

It is much easier to give advice than to accept and follow it. As I reach the end of my life's journey, I offer some final thoughts.

In the old days, when the merit system was always being

attacked, on trial, and threatened, it needed support. The system has never been perfect, but it has survived.

There is no one way to administer a merit system, but there must be honesty, truth, and sincerity on both sides of any question. I do not have in mind, therefore, that there is one, and only one, best adn precise form of personnel administration and no other that should be established. Our present laws are better than our best possible administration of them. One does one's duty when one does well everything the law permits. If the laws need to be changed, everyone knows the procedure.

Many years ago, Alexander Pope wrote: "For forms of government, let fools contest. What'ere is best administered is best." Thousands of people in thousands of ways, including innumerable books, have tried to improve upon what Pope wrote. None has succeeded. For my part, I would discontinue the Civil Service Commission form of personnel organization. Instead, I would place the public personnel system under a director with cabinet-level status, and clothe him with the authority to do the job.

The Future

Of the future, I am hopeful, but I am not too confident. I have little sympathy with those youngsters who behave foolishly, who talk about the gap between them and their parents. Discipline, and not indulgence, should have been and must be the motto. These children will be our leaders tomorrow. They will set the standards and raise their own children. Too many of them, I am afraid, have gathered scars in their silly and dangerous actions in pursuit of what they call their new freedom that will trouble them for life. We have lost a great deal of strength and majesty of our country. It will take us a long time to get back to the standards that have been our pride and distinction.

Our task here is to recapture some of that old dedication and concern for better standards of conduct in public administration and in all that we do.

In prosperous times, many people do not want to enter the public service because of its limitations. I suspect that the time will come again when many people will seek public service employment. Assurance of that employment, the higher pay, and greater fringe benefits and the dignity of working for the people, will bring this about.

We should be concerned always in having industrious, devoted, and able public employees. Their work will be reflected in better government and that is always a first consideration.

We cannot live in the old political, grasping way and remain the great and strong nation we want to be and must be, as the example to the world of a democracy with all its freedoms and individual opportunities. Vigilance and determination will assure this. We know that our government must keep step with our needs if we are to remain a great country. Good personnel, fairly treated, properly organized and directed, and properly paid, and where all shall work for the state and none for self, alone is the answer.

We have celebrated recently our nation's two hundredth anniversary. The wrecks of empires strewn along the path of history are a forceful reminder of their death. Let us not forget the words of Benjamin Franklin when he said to the Continental Congress: "You have a government, if you can keep it." He was saying that we could lose that government by neglect, from the inside, not by conquest by an outside enemy. Our aim, our safety, and our very existence, will depend on what we do within our government. We must think on these things.

Retrospection

When asked what I consider to be the most noteworthy accomplishment of my career as a civil servant, I believe it is the fixing of the place and the part of the personnel system in government and the proper place and the authority of its director. Along with this, I believe that I have always demonstrated the truth of my convictions about the whole personnel system.

Several years ago, Mr. William Druz, then Director of the State of New Jersey Department of Personnel Management, expressed an interest in developing a history of the New Jersey civil service system. His findings represent a capsule of my life's work, so I offer them here as a review of that history. Mr. Druz stated:

> I have been going into the records of the history of personnel management. I find your fingerprints in a great many places in New Jersey and elsewhere. Back in 1922, you were President of the Civil Service Assembly; you were acting as a consultant to legislative committees and commissions; you were writing state papers of all kinds; you were somewhere, and usually in the vanguard, in every important city and state movement; you took over the records of the Civil Service Assembly after the Black Monday of '29, and became its President for three more years. When your Bureau had to close down, you were a member of all kinds of organizations related to governmental procedures; you were chairman of the Board of Tourist Development; you were an educator of note and lectured throughout the country; you were a banker, a farmer, and many other things; and you have served as executive assistant to the Governors. You stood out in all of these activities to one governor after another, wrote their speeches, messages, and did countless other things for them.

"What was your secret?" he asked. My answer was: "I don't know." Something inside me, I suppose, helped me carry the burdens, that drove me to work. I had worked hard all of my life. It was not vanity, nor money, nor publicity. Rather, I suppose, it was an innate desire to help people, and to know somehow that people would be able to say: "I am better because he passed this way."

CHAPTER 5

Toward a More Effective
*Public Administration**

Mr. Chairman and friends, As I have been listening to this animated conversation around me, I am reluctant to interpose some of my own comments that may not be of much interest to you. When Ken Warner asked me what I should like to talk about, I said about fifteen minutes. I make no promises, for I have a great deal to say to you.

I am somewhat in the position of the young trainee in one of these new enterprises here in Washington. He had not gotten far into his training course when his principal found himself unable to keep a speaking engagement. He sent the trainee as the only substitute available at the time. The young man was a serious chap. He wanted to make good, but he was somewhat overwhelmed by an assignment so soon after he had begun his training. He went to the meeting and when he was called upon to speak, nervous and excited, he began by saying: "I came here to make a speech, you came here to listen. If you get through before I do, kindly get up and walk out quietly." Perhaps you will stay with me all the way.

* Address at the 60th Annual Conference of the Public Personnel Association, Washington, D.C., October 26, 1966.

An organization that has been in business for sixty years is bound to have a few antiques. I came to show you younger members what you may look like after fifty-six years of continuing membership. I have brought with me a second exhibit, a man whose fingerprints are all over the pages of the history of this association. Fred Telford is somewhat my junior as to his membership status, but he is not exactly a young man either. More than any other man he has helped me in working out the plans and program for the Bureau of Public Personnel Administration on the basis of which we were able to get financial support and start this association, then the National Civil Service Assembly, rolling. He was the first appointee in the Bureau and the real founder of your secretariat. From a loosely organized group of people, prospecting around trying to find its place in the public administrative picture, and nearly falling apart, he became quickly the major factor in drawing the Assembly together, giving it a goal and a purpose and starting it in its thinking and planning ahead. In the ten years Fred served the Bureau and the Assembly, he worked, and planned, and travelled as Ken Warner does today, giving encouragement where it was needed, helping to solve the pertinent problems and leading the way in the personnel field.

Working together, Telford and I did make progress, but we had a long way to go, in spite of the obstacles put in our way; and they were many and very real. With little and uncertain public support and constant political sniping, we managed to stay alive, and with a lot of toil and sweat a little group of us hammered out the tools of the trade that you use today as a matter of course. I am quite sure many people since then believe that they did these things, but that does not concern us. We were looking for the way that we must travel, what we could do to carry forward the aims and purpose in which we were engaged.

There was a time when we believed in the authority that said "The young men shall see visions and the old men shall dream dreams." And you would probably expect me to spend my time telling about our dreams. I am not going to do that. I am reversing the order, for meeting the problems of today is a much more important matter than telling our dreams. I came to this meeting because I like to be with personnel people and because I want to make some observations on what I think I see ahead. I have been doing this sort of thing for some fifty years, from time to time. Sometimes I have been right.

I have read and re-read your Committee Report on Future Goals of this Public Personnel Association, and President Stahl's Letter of Transmittal. They are both significant documents. They lay down some of the guidelines and stake out the landmarks that you will do well to follow. We have had other plans before and the proposals in this report are not new to me. They follow much the same general plans of our earlier days. We had visions, too. We realized some of them. The problems you face are much greater in size and complexity than ours were. We were pioneering. Great changes have taken place since that time and it is wise for you now to undertake to list these problems in their seeming order of importance and in their present-day setting. Much as you have done, I think you are a little late about the progress you have made. I bid you make haste now and do not give up until you get more of the things accomplished that are not yet done and are necessary to our further progress.

I concur completely in what you say about the work of Ken Warner and his devoted staff. He and they have done a remarkable job. Ken has built the kind of organization I dreamed about. He has done this by reason of his ability and his tireless devotion. He has been so kind to me as to say more than once that I was helping him along the way. If we personnel people really know anything worthwhile, and I think we do, that knowledge and expertise is centered in this Association.

If real progress is to be made in the years immediately ahead in public administration, and particularly in personnel management, it must be sparked by you. My word to all of you and all that you represent is to get to work and don't stop until you have made your mark, as those of us have done and those who come after you will do. Make no little plans. Little things do not appeal. Think big but straight, and don't be turned aside by dim mirages of opposition and unidentified objects or objectives. I want to see the Executive Council and you experienced leaders in the personnel field give your secretariat your help and support in putting this membership to work on the great number of pressing and difficult problems that you are facing. But let me observe, in passing, that lack of complaint is not always a measure of progress. It is the restless ones who help most and they sometimes have ideas and plans that will work. Gadflies have their uses.

I can't cover the entire Report now. I do want to comment, however, on three or four of the items therein by way of emphasis.

1. Your proposal that the Association should be the official voice for the personnel function interests me. None of your memories take you back to the time I began to talk about this same thing. I was trying to sell the idea that we should develop these "principles, concepts, standards, and sound practices" you mention. I proposed that we should set up these standards, factor by factor, part by part, until we had covered the whole of personnel administration as we then conceived it, including management. I proposed that we publish what we believed in and that we stand by it come what may. Some starts were made but we did not get very far and as management changed in the secretariat and Assembly, it took off in different and easier directions. Let me urge you now to turn aside from that practice. Stick to the things we know. They are right. They are the bases upon which you must build.

After sixty years there are no really established standards in which you as an Association believe in fully or have adopted and followed. There is plenty of advice about every factor in the personnel process, but no single set of standards, and there are none to speak with the determination and authority that is needed.

I sometimes think we should blame ourselves. We have a fever for rushing into print at every opportunity. The slogan, "publish or perish," has struck here as in every other field, and the product of this policy flows from the presses in constantly increasing volume. This Association, if it is to be the spokesman, must set its own standards rather than accept somebody's or everybody's procedures, ways, vocabulary and the like. When the secretariat is asked for advice on how to do this or that or the other thing by an anxious inquirer, reference to the so-called literature in the field confuses more than it clarifies. When we are asked what is the way to do something involving procedure or any job in personnel administration, we must be able and willing to give the answer — the official answer. It must be the right answer and we must stand by it. Follow this line and inquiring people wanting help will recognize you as the spokesmen in the field. You will not have to claim the place.

When we began to bring some order out of the confusion in our field, there was considerable talk about the question of whether those engaged in personnel work were practicing a science or an art. I was never troubled about that matter; I just wanted to get along with the job, to develop standards and improve our product. But if a science is a body of classified knowledge, we are not practicing a science. Too many of you are devising your own programs, using and advocating new approaches to the same problems. We can and we must follow the correct standards. We of my generation did that. We laid the foundations, we proved them in practice, and they must be written down. We should have manuals or handbooks covering every important factor involved in our practice of the personnel function as complete and as accurate as, for example, an engineer's handbook. Fred Telford, who is only a memory to most of you, was working on such a manual when he failed in health.

Wherever one turns he faces problems that need to be met. There is a lot of foundation money looking for worthwhile projects. A higher level in, and a more effective, public administration is certainly one of our great problems. I believe that funds can be had in sizeable volume if we try hard enough. I urge you to make a try in this direction.

2. Another problem that must be met is test and testings. As you know, the merit principle for the public service was built around a formal examination procedure expressed and emphasized in early civil service statutes; "Keep the rascals out" was the watchword. The rascals were supposed to be ignorant, the

examination would do the trick. It helped, but it did not bring the answer. It did provide an opportunity for people seeking public employment, but times have changed. People no longer seek government work in sufficient numbers even, and the personnel agency must go out seeking qualified people. The time that must elapse under the old order, when you get a prospect and when he can be put to work, is no longer feasible. Decisions must be made at once.

In addition to these difficulties, we do not yet know what constitutes a meaningful test — a proper measurement of qualifications and fitness. We know how to validate tests. That is a costly and laborious process. We have but a handful of such tests even now available, and notwithstanding the claims made by many people, no general test has yet been devised. In my opinion, at least, that will bring the results desired quickly and surely. At any rate the selection and appointment of workers and professionals of all classes in the public service is due for revolutionary changes, and we must do something about this matter. The answer to this problem will not wait. Here, too, is a place for a comprehensive and exhaustive study under a liberal foundation grant.

3. Another matter of great importance is employer-employee relations: This all-important matter of employer-employee relations should probably be placed first on every list of problems facing those in the field of personnel and public administration today. We are all caught up in a period of revolutionary change that has spread throughout the world. It is universal and it touches every governmental jurisdiction and unit in this nation, and that of every member-nation whose officers and workers are part of the membership of this organization. We are so accustomed to crises in these days that one more seems to be just another incident and nothing to get excited about, but these problems will not go away. They must be faced.

Again, "employee rights" has become a much talked about subject. It seems that our whole population is talking about human rights. We have suddenly discovered that government employees and workers in all classes and groups are deprived people — second-class citizens. To me this is silly. I am no second-class citizen; neither are any of you nor is any public worker. Those who use this term, or any other disparaging terms or language about an employee or his work, may weaken the employee's image and make him dissatisfied.

I have spent most of my working life in the public service. I have been overworked by choice, and underpaid, in part at least by my own choosing, because I believed there were more important considerations than either work or pay in what I was trying to do. I don't recommend that you do as I did, but self-pity has no place here. I would not change my life's work if I could. I think many of you men and women have something of the same feeling about your public service. We are privileged citizens because we serve. There are some hardships for many public workers, of course, but their lot has been greatly improved in recent years and there is more ahead for them.

I want to see even justice for every worker in the public service or in other fields. I want him paid well, treated with consideration by his directing officers, provided with suitable working conditions, given proper privileges and adequate machinery for hearing of his grievances when he has grievances that should be heard. I want him to remember always, though, that he has responsibilities as well as rights and that those rights do not extend to actions that endanger the health and safety of others. I want him to remember, too, that he is a part of government and what he says and what he does has a far-reaching effect on his own image and that of his fellow workers.

There is no place for work stoppages in the public service. We have them every day, and too many people have not thought this matter through to its end results. A government that cannot or does not have the respect of its citizens, and does not or cannot enforce its own laws, cannot long continue. No form of government has yet been devised that will permit every citizen to do as he pleases. It is not just old fashioned to declare that we have had in our country for these long years a good form of government. It is not perfect but it is better than any other type extant. Under it we have prospered more than any nation in recorded history. It is folly for any individual or group to try to weaken it.

Certainly we have many problems but let us seek to be a part of the answers, not a part of the problems. I raise this question for it must be one of great concern to both personnel and administrators. We have been sowing the wind, the whirlwind may be coming near.

4. "National and local government relations" is another problem that must give us all concern, namely that of our relations as an agency and the national civil service commission. For a great many years I, in common with others having to do with Public Personnel Association activities, have been trying to devise ways and means of getting a closer relationship between those of us who work and think at the federal level and those who work and think at the state and local level. In my time these relationships were always friendly and understanding, but in recent years, the national government has entered upon so many new undertakings, and all governments have grown so fast in worker needs, in extended activities, and cooperative undertakings that you, now on the firing line, find a great deal of your work and many of your problems are involved in these joint undertakings. Too many agencies, groups, and people in the public service are doing the same things in our great and complicated bureaucracy. Possibly the greatest problem that government has, so far as its administration is concerned, is simplifying to reduce that duplication.

I mention this subject with no thought of raising debate or contention, but I do so merely because I know, periodically, every one of you must seek solutions satisfactory to both parties in interest that will work. I believe we have drawn apart rather than getting closer together. You see it in your conferences, such as this, that count. Those who work at the national level are interested in matters discussed at that level. Those who serve at the state and local levels gravitate to the meetings where their problems and procedures are discussed. The suggestion you raise in your Report is that there should be more regional, area, or special meetings and fewer general, national or international meetings. To me that in itself seems to indicate that you have been thinking about this matter. I think that sort of thinking is wise and constructive.

You have in your present membership a great many members at the national level, but a majority, I should suppose, are from local government levels. One cannot expect the first interest of all to follow from one to the other. That interest will follow, usually, its own governmental level. I suggest you consider holding some conferences by governmental level rather than on a strictly geographical basis. I have a notion you will increase the values of your meetings in that way.

5. "Competent workers" represent another condition that we now have and that will continue if we are able to keep our managed economy on an even keel. I speak of the shortage of help in nearly every class or type of work in practically every government big and little in the country. This, too, tends to draw us apart even though we keep talking about cooperation. We are all after our part of the available people. We are in competition with each other. We must act this way if we hope to succeed in filling our own personnel needs. I believe we must recognize this situation and, for the present at least, go our separate ways accepting the inherent added costs and disadvantages. As an example, we may look to the field of education. I read within the past few weeks a report on the shortage of teachers in several of the states. Almost without exception, spokesmen in the field pointed to the fact that the number of teachers needed in their respective states was almost exactly equal to the number of teachers of the state now employed by federal or welfare agencies. In these efforts to widen and extend the general welfare, we create an imbalance in one activity to set up another. And who shall say that it is wise to weaken our public educational system by taking away trained teachers for new undertakings and experiments in state versus national government.

Although I have already talked too much and said too little, I ask you to bear with me a little further. I want to say something about the unfortunate trends toward the building of a giant national government at the expense of state and local governments. This is contrary to all of our thinking and philosophy in America. Our government was established and has grown beyond our greatest hopes on the principle of a balance of powers by divisions at the federal level, and as between the states and the national governments. Personally, I think this change to the extent it has gone, and is going, is unfortunate, but I do not propose to enter into a discussion of the matter here. I am concerned with the problems that these changes have precipitated with respect to the personnel function.

6. With respect to these numerous grants directly from the national treasury to the states and directly through the states to local governments big and little, the national agencies must lay down the rules for the use and expenditure of the moneys and supervise the procedures. The local personnel agency is expected, even required, to perform its part of the operating functions. There are many conflicts as to policy and procedures going on continually that do neither of these levels any good. I have just read one such memorandum from one of our large jurisdictions urging changes in requirements laid down that cannot be met. Again, this way of doing business lowers the place and the image of local personnel systems and leads the people to believe that local government fails in all things and that they must look to Washington for relief and direction. Money talks even though it is our money, whether it is paid to the local, state, city or county where the work is to be done or is sent to Washington where it, or part of it, comes back to us from there. The expense of that procedure is costly in the extreme.

We need to keep remembering that the genius of our way of life is built around our notions of state and local governments. And our history, all history I think, shows very clearly that improvement in public affairs grows up. It is not, and cannot be, handed down. We yet have states and cities, counties, villages and boroughs, and their governments are in fruitful and familiar soil.

As I have noted above, personnel people place their first

interest in the level in which they work. This centralization extends, it does not shorten, the gap between. The field in which the Public Personnel Association has worked for the most part, and in which it has had the greatest effect, is in and with state and local jurisdictions. In my judgment it is yet there. The federal agencies have the personnel, the funds, and the talent to work out their own procedures, and they will do these things. They do not require Public Personnel Association help and they are not likely to accept it. Local governments are not in that fortunate position, and they need help.

Again, great as our federal government has grown, state and local governments have twice as many civil servants and spend very much more money on their personnel than does the federal government. Local government is yet big business and if there is to be improvement in public administration, and there must be, it must develop from within. It cannot be handed down.

I am strongly convinced that the plan now proposed to give federal money directly to state and local personnel agencies is wrong. This is not the way to strengthen local personnel agencies. They serve their own jurisdictions, they should and can be supported at home. It is, indeed, a strange world when a chairman bred in New England where local government was born in America, and is yet an effective institution, should find himself so far away from his native philosophy.

I agree that this is a new day. I know that changes must be made in any institution to meet new conditions. I believe we have waited too long, and now we are going too fast. Evolution, not revolution, is what has been and is yet needed. Maybe I see things ahead that are not really there and that in some way or other we shall come through. But at the very best luck we can expect, even with the greatest possible effort you and your helpers can put forth, the way to be difficult and calls for more industry, more devotion, and more wisdom than we have heretofore demonstrated. The years I have lived prevent my participation in this great adventure. I envy you your opportunity in it.

My last word is stay together in interest and in spirit. There is no greater task than that now before you.

Above the facade of the Temple of Justice in Sacramento

is carved the legend: "Give Me Men to Match My Mountains." The mountains are tall and rough. Tall men have conquered them. The problems ahead of you are of mountain size. Only tall men are equal to their solution. May you and all you represent have the stature, the wisdom, the dedication and the endurance to do the job.

CHAPTER 6

*Moving into the Third Century of the Republic**

Dr. O. Glenn Stahl's Introduction:

One of our members in opening this series of brief presentations said that she had experienced professionally one-fifth of the two-hundred years of the span of life of our American government in its present form. I am now about to introduce an individual whose total life span expends over almost one-half of the two-hundred years of that period, a truly distinguished citizen of North America.

Dr. Charles P. Messick was working at the personnel function before almost everyone else in this room was born. He has had experience in the field of education as a teacher, a member and president of a city Board of Education for many years. He never went to high school. In the business world he has been a member of the corporate boards of important institutions, such as the Prudential Life Insurance Company, a billion-dollar bank, and a number of other social and economic institutions and agen-

---

* Address at the 70th Annual Meeting of the International Personnel Management Association (formerly the Public Personnel Association), Washington, D.C., December 2, 1976.

cies. He is also a writer and lecturer known throughout America. He has two B.A.s, two masters, three doctorates, and other types of recognition throughout America and beyond.

He began his work in the personnel management field in the State of New Jersey as early as 1909. He was a leader in those days, and he continues as a leader to this day. He turned the merit system in the State of New Jersey from a negative factor of examinations, which had little if any value in the selection of qualified workers in the public service, to an effective, positive system, demonstrated its value and success, and in his work there laid the pattern for America that is followed to this day.

Dr. Messick was president of this Association, then called The Civil Service Assembly of the United States and Canada, on two different occasions. He was president in 1922 and 1923 and again in 1931, 1932 and 1933, during the dark days of the depression when America and most of the world were shocked into idleness and distress. In addition to many other duties to the state and nation, he took over the records and responsibilities of this organization and saved it from dissolution — all this besides his activities as leader, planner, chairman, secretary and counselor to governors, to civic groups, and as planner and inspired leader and aide to practically all public agencies. In reading the record of those days, it seems impossible that anyone could stand up under the load he carried. When I asked him how he did it, his answer was, "I don't know, I did what I could."

Added to this, Dr. Messick was and is a lecturer and a writer known throughout America. During the last three years he has produced three volumes: *An Adventure In Public Personnel Administration* in 1973; *The Principles of Public Personnel Administration* in 1976, and *The Passing Scene, A Commentary on Public Affairs* also in 1976, and he tells me he is working on a fourth book that he has not yet named. These recent works, while drawing to some extent upon some of his earlier writings, have all been carefully supplemented and edited by the wisdom of the ages that only a Charles P. Messick could bring to the subject. I am delighted and honored to have the opportunity to present to the members of this organization one of the Godfathers of public personnel administration, Charles P. Messick.

Dr. Messick's Address

Mr. Chairman, friends and fellow associates, It is a great privilege for me to be here during this annual meeting, to renew acquaintances, to talk to many of you about your problems and to listen. I cannot but be pleased for the kind words of Dr. Stahl in presenting me. He has been more than kind. He is my long-time, valued, friend. He has gone through all the way I have traveled, noted my landmarks and guidelines and created new ones to mark as guides for those yet active and those who will come after them as the changing times require.

You can see that I am in no fit condition to talk long enough to complete what I have planned to say. I have had this cold for some days and I have been unable to get the best of it. It seems to be winning. In anticipating such a difficulty, I have written down what I hoped to say to you. I have asked Doctor Stahl to read it for me.

(Dr. Stahl: Charlie, I'm more than delighted to have this opportunity to convey your words to this group; and I shall do so as faithful as I possibly can. Let me say that in the very first sentence he mentions my name, but this is quite incidental to the point that he makes. I am now reading from Dr. Messick's address.)

Some months ago, Dr. Stahl came to visit me at my home in Delaware. We talked about many things. For the most part we discussed your large and important organization, its purposes, its principles, its programs and its progress. Through the years I have followed its development by reading your journal and other printed material you have issued to your members. The last time I spoke at an annual meeting of this Association was ten years ago on your sixtieth birthday, so it was natural for Dr. Stahl and me to discuss the principles upon which this organization was established, which I helped to forge in the years of its beginning, and which are landmarks and guidelines, as he put it, of "the eternal verities of public personnel administration." The result of that meeting brings me here once again, not only to talk to you, but to learn from your members and your speakers and to renew acquaintances.

To undertake to talk about the "eternal verities" of this or any organization is a bit pretentious for me as for anyone; and age alone does not confer on me a license to speak for the edification or the guidance of others, nor does it extend to me the right to tell you how to conduct the affairs of this Association. But this bicentennial year is a time of retrospection and reflection, not only for our nation's founding principles, its past, and its destiny. It is your anniversary as well, your seventieth, and you are giving consideration to your own progress, and making plans for your future.

During the period of your existence you have made progress. I have followed that progress every step of the way. I saw you organized. I knew many of that little group of civil service commissioners who came together in 1906 to talk about their common problems and became the seedbed of this Association — some of that same group who, as young people, were among those who organized the original National Civil Service Reform League.

I was alive when the Pendleton Act, the first merit system act enacted in America, was passed in 1883. I have lived through all of these movements and almost half of the time that America itself was a free government.

I entered the field of personnel management in 1909 as a special examiner, advanced to the executive head of the Division of Civil Service in New Jersey in 1917, and retired from that office in 1949, but I have continued my interest in personnel until today.

Merely being alive is not enough, however. Seneca, an old Roman philosopher, wrote two thousand years ago: "Nothing is more disgraceful than when one who is old should have nothing to say but his years." I do not accept that axiom either.

If I am truthful, I am obliged to say that I have had more influence in the development of this Association from its beginning than any other person. Others followed me and accepted that leadership. What I did in New Jersey became the pattern for the whole of America and continues as such to this day. I am the parent of this organization to the extent that anyone can have that relationship to an organization.

Those of you who are old enough will remember that I

was the moving spirit of every significant advance made in the creation and practice of personnel management in my fifty years of service. I have continued my interest and my service as a consultant and in recent years as a writer in the personnel management field.

If all that has gone before is prologue and is to be erased and of no account so far as the present and future is concerned, then all our efforts heretofore have been useless, and we must start again from the beginning. But I do not accept that dictum. I believe, I know, that the past has an almost determining influence on the present, and that the past and the present do determine in very large measure the future. Nor does the fact that because something has been done before, or that the age of a policy or person has some controlling adverse influence on what we think or do now, mean anything but foolishness. It has always been my plan to do something constructive, something that would improve or add to any progress upon which I was working.

I spoke at your annual meeting ten years ago. I promised then that I would come again in ten years. I am here. I will not tell you when, if at all, I will come again, but I can assure you that I will follow your progress and your growth and your power and your service as the years pass.

I have always worked under pressure, but at last that pressure is off. Yet, I don't know how to be idle and carefree, whatever that may mean. I yet work for exercise. I write in the evening. I have written a book a year for the past three years on various phases of personnel management. These books are available to you in your headquarters office and in many state libraries throughout the country.

Notwithstanding the fact that I have a time limit that must be respected I cannot resist the temptation to say a few words, a warning if you will permit, to us and to everybody whom we have selected by election or authorized appointment to do our public business for us, about the staggering public debt under which we live both in the states, their subdivisions, and the nation itself. These debts threaten our very existence; yet, a great proportion of our population has little or no concern about them. Some of our governments have reached the point of no return and acknowledge their bankrupt condition. New York City, for instance, has acknowledged that it cannot pay its debts; and many more are trembling on the brink. Our national credit is weakened and many of our cities and local areas are in danger. It doesn't require unusual wisdom to see and even understand this situation. Warnings have come to us from the very beginning of America as a nation, and of late years they are repeated in the news media almost every day.

Jefferson's pen was hardly dry from writing our national charter when he wrote: "I place economy among the first and most important virtues and public debt as the greatest danger to be feared. To preserve our independence, we must not let our rulers lead us into debt under the pretense of caring for them."

Jefferson saw the dangers ahead. Franklin warned us against debts. Washington warned us against debt and foreign entanglements. Economists, scholars, citizens, all have repeated these warnings, but to no effect. Day after day, year after year, we know but we fail to act. We are in danger, but do nothing except add to our public indebtedness, which will probably never be paid.

President Hoover wrote: "If you really want to make the world over again, try the word 'old' for a while. There are some old things that made this country. There is the old virtue of religious faith. There is the virtue of incorruptible service and honor in public office. There is the virtue of thrift and individual liberty . . . There is love of country and willingness to sacrifice for it." But the next day, after his last day in office, the era of "tax and tax, spend and spend" began. It has continued until today, and we are promised more tomorrow.

It is not fantasy for me or anyone to talk in this way. This practice is a fact, and I repeat it is dangerous. We know the consequences, but no one of those of our people who sit in high places has had the internal fortitude to stop or even reduce this threat to our nation and the people. Our welfare and our endurance is yet in our own hands. We are yet the most powerful nation the world has ever seen. We have all the facilities to hold that position, but we now have competition, and we must keep that in mind always.

I realize that I have violated every rule of speechmaking by talking about unrelated subjects. My excuse is that no one can cover a subject, it would require a book to do that. In the short time allotted to me I have tried to touch a few high spots in the matters of most importance to all of us, to our country, and to the world. As I complete my writing and my speaking with this effort, I have only a feeling of regret that a field where there is so much to do, I have done so little.

My last words to you are: You have done well thus far. Your greater problems are before you, more difficult, more complicated, and almost impossible of solution. I hope that you will continue to observe and use the principles that we developed in the early years and use the tools we fashioned in their solution. They are the same now as they were at the beginning — the eternal verities of personnel management.

CHAPTER 7

An Epilogue with Verse

Dr. Lyman Abbott (1835-1922) was a leading Congregational clergyman. He succeeded the renowned Henry Ward Beecher as pastor of the Plymouth Church in Brooklyn and served in that capacity for eleven years. He also served as editor of the popular weekly news magazine, *The Outlook,* for forty years.

One of his last published stories was entitled "The End of the Journey," a composition of the highest quality and one, in my opinion, that has never been excelled. Because this brief but moving composition so well expresses my own sentiments at this juncture in my own long life, I consider it appropriate to repeat it here.*

"The pilgrim had come a long way and the fatigue of the journey was in his face and the stains of it on his garments. He walked slowly and painfully and in his steps were the record of many leagues of travel. Far behind as he travelled on was the last ray of the morning light, once gloriously glad over all the earth, now like the last ray of a sun that had long set.

---

* Although I have searched the many issues of *The Outlook* for the years 1914 through 1922, the year he died, I have been unable to find the correct citation of this composition. I assume, however, it appears in one of those issues of that magazine.

"For a long time now he had travelled alone, for the little band that had set out with him had vanished silently, one by one, from his side as he moved on in the gathering darkness.

"And, when the mists of the morning had passed came noonday with its heat, its quickening activity and its deepening experience, and after noonday evening. And so long had he been lonely it seemed to him that he had always been alone and it had always been dark. For some time now he had no sense of movement except in the changing landscape and this was contrary to his very nature, for in his youth the fountain of pity seemed irresistible and in later years when surcease from sorrow came, the fountain would rise and send a gush of joy to his heart. For a long time now there had been no movement of the waters. Age had touched all that he possessed, and so moving slowly he came late one dark night to the gate that closes the road.

"He knocked feebly with trembling fingers. The gate opened on noiseless hinges, and no one stood beside the gate for it marked neither the beginning nor the end of the journey. No sound was heard, no sign was visible, but a soft light lay over the landscape and he saw without seeing that nature bloomed there in unfulfilled loveliness and he heard without hearing the song of birds that had ne'er been hushed by wintry skies. The pilgrim entered within the gate, and as he sat he saw that fading and wearing away of his garments affected only his garments. Once more young but with a wisdom greater than youth, and as he rose the pain disappeared from his body and the ache from his limbs. He moved on with quickened steps, for in the mists ahead he saw beautiful forms moving and heard familiar voices coming out of his childhood and his heart grew sick with joy at the sound of them."

Only a great and good man could have composed that story. The press, magazines, books and other news media are filled with very different kinds of stories — stories of suffering and sacrifice of people from youth through old age. Loyalty, bravery, and sacrifice are neither new characteristics of our people and time, nor of other peoples and eras. Examples surround us every day.

There is a second story fraught with great significance to me that is so familiar that I will forego repeating it here. It is the story of Henry Stanley searching for and finding David Livingstone in the depths of Africa. Livingstone refused to return to civilization with Stanley. According to Stanley's account of their parting, Livingstone, looking over the vast expanse of jungle and surrounded by the natives whom he had served, in a trembling voice and with tears in his eyes, murmured to himself: "So much to do and so little time."

I repeat those fateful words with humility and with some small measure of hope that what I have tried to do has helped others and will serve to help those who follow. As I look around and consider the condition of mankind, I see so much that should be done, so much unfinished business on the agenda of the future. "So much to do and so little time." As I fade into the shadows, I hope that it can be said of me: "He did what he could."

There is a verse with which I end this book. I do not remember its title. Nor do I know who composed it. Perhaps I did. In any event, it appears a reflective conclusion to these reflections of a public servant.

> The twilight falls on the chapel walls
> Where the twining ivy clings,
> And my steps are slow
> As I onward go,
> But the song in my heart still sings,
> Yes, the song in my heart still sings.
>
> Hark to the bells,
> How their clear notes tell
> Of the deeds of the day that is gone
> They ring out fair on the summer air,
> Recalling the deeds that are done.
> Yes, they tell of the things that are done.

There is quiet now
As we stand beside
The road that leads down the hill.
And memory alone nerves the sinews and bones
As I raise the old flag still.
Yes, I carry the old banner still.

Down that gentle slope,
With its peace and its hope,
I will ramble the rest of the way.
And I'll sit in the sun
Till the light is gone
And it comes to the end of the day.
Yes, I am nearing the end of the day.